Walking Eye
mobile app

Discover the world's best destinations with the Insight Guides Walking Eye app, available to download for free in the App Store and Google Play.

The container app provides easy access to fantastic free content on events and activities taking place in your current location or chosen destination, with the possibility of booking, as well as the regularly-updated Insight Guides travel blog: Inspire Me. In addition, you can purchase curated, premium destination guides through the app, which feature local highlights, hotel, bar, restaurant and shopping listings, an A to Z of practical information and more. Or purchase and download Insight Guides eBooks straight to your device.

Available on the **App Store**

Get it on **Google play**

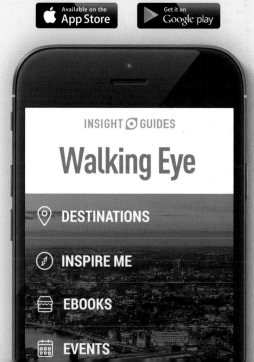

INSIGHT ⊙ GUIDES

Walking Eye

⊙ DESTINATIONS

⊘ INSPIRE ME

⊜ EBOOKS

▦ EVENTS

TOP 10 ATTRACTIONS

SHAKALAND
Immerse yourself in the Zulu way of life.
See page 56.

TABLE MOUNTAIN
Its breathtaking views
complete a visit to Cape Town.
See page 73.

OUDTSHOORN
Ostrich mania in the Little Karoo.

TWO OCEANS AQUARIUM
Marine life close up on
Cape Town's waterfront.

KRUGER NATIONAL PARK
One of Africa's truly great wildlife sanctuaries and a top destination for big game viewing. See page 41.

CAPE POINT
Look out from the far south of Africa. See page 78.

UKHAHLAMBA-DRAKENSBERG PARK
A must-visit for spectacular views of South Africa's largest mountain range. See page 47.

THE BLUE TRAIN
View South Africa's astonishing scenery from its luxurious carriages. See page 82.

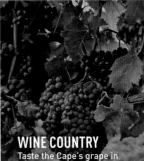

PLETTENBERG BAY
This classic arc of sandy beach is one highlight of South Africa's vast golden coastline. See page 63.

WINE COUNTRY
Taste the Cape's grape in Paarl and Stellenbosch. See page 79.

A **PERFECT** TOUR

Arrival

Arrive in Johannesburg and fly to Kruger Mpumalanga Airport, 45 minutes away. Transfer to a private game lodge in Sabi Sands Reserve, adjacent to Kruger National Park. The luxurious Inyathi Game Lodge (see page 134), in the western sector of the reserve, is a good option. Arrive in time for lunch, followed by an afternoon game drive.

Game reserve

Spend the day at the game reserve. You may be lucky enough to see the Big 5 in just one day – not to mention zebra, hippo and giraffe. Don't miss the chance to embark on an atmospheric night drive, where you'll see smaller creatures like porcupine and civet as well.

Garden Route

From Johannesburg, fly to George, in the heart of the Garden Route. Hire a car and drive the 50km (34 miles) to Knysna. This bustling holiday resort is located on a picturesque lagoon, the ideal spot to try your hand at angling or sailing. Stay overnight in a luxury tree house at the Phantom Forest Lodge (see page 138).

Jo'burg or Pretoria

Return to Johannesburg, where you can get a fix of South African history at the MuseuMAfricA and enjoy the shops and hotels of upmarket Sandton. Alternatively, opt for nearby capital city Pretoria – beautiful even when its famous jacaranda trees are not in bloom.

Day 5

Beach break

Drive to the seaside town of Plettenberg Bay and relax on one of Plett's beautiful white-sand beaches, take a guided tour at primate rescue centre Monkeyland, or ride a pachyderm at the Elephant Sanctuary. Stay overnight at the Grand Café and Rooms (see page 138) for a touch of quirky opulence.

Day 7

Townships and Table Mountain

In the morning, take the cable car up Table Mountain and marvel at the panoramic views of Cape Town. Spend the afternoon on a township tour: you will learn how the majority of South Africa's population lives, and the residents will benefit from your support.

Day 8

Winelands

Take a day trip to the Winelands. After you've sampled the rich reds and crisp whites at Môreson wine estate, you'll be ready for lunch at Bread & Wine restaurant (see page 107). Stay overnight in lovely Franschoek and have dinner at Le Quartier Francais (see page 109). The following day, fly out of Cape Town.

Day 6

Arrive in Cape Town

Drive to Cape Town, just over 400km (265 miles) away, and head to the V&A Waterfront. After you have set up base at your hotel, it's time to visit the top-class aquarium or go shopping for souvenirs. Then while the evening away at the many restaurants and bars.

CONTENTS

INTRODUCTION

With remarkably diverse scenery, innumerable species of large mammals and birds, a rich floral kingdom and a cultural heritage rooted in three different continents, the Republic of South Africa, once known for its racial segregation, has evolved into one of the world's top tourist destinations.

A large number of international carriers fly direct to the country and, if you happen to be travelling from the UK, you'll avoid jetlag, as South Africa is just two hours ahead of gmt. A non-stop flight from London to Johannesburg – around 9,700km (6,000 miles) – takes about 11 hours. Direct flights to Durban or Cape Town take an hour or two longer.

While South Africa is the undisputed powerhouse of the African continent, with massive industrial and mining enterprises, a truly astonishing range of natural landscapes awaits the visitor: vast stretches of savannah brimming with herds

Sea Point Beach, Cape Town

of big game, wide bays and palm-lined beaches, a colourful diversity of wildflowers, towering rock amphitheatres, evergreen forests and semi-desert, vineyards and orchards. This variation is also reflected in the architecture, from Zulu beehive huts (which look like mudand-thatch igloos) to gracefully

Seeing South Africa

An excellent way to explore South Africa would be to hire a car (see page 114). Driving is on the left and English is spoken throughout the country. South Africans are keen travellers in their own land and expect high standards, so facilities are generally excellent.

whitewashed Cape Dutch mansions to the towering skyscrapers of central Johannesburg.

GEOGRAPHY AND CLIMATE

South Africa's coastline stretches for 2,500km (1,600 miles) from the desert border with Namibia on the Atlantic coast, down around the tip of the continent and up to subtropical Mozambique beside the Indian Ocean. The coastal belt is mostly narrow, separated from the high inland plateau by a mountainous escarpment. Inland, South Africa borders Botswana, Zimbabwe and Swaziland, and surrounds the 30,355-sq km (11,720-sq mile) independent Kingdom of Lesotho.

Officially classified as semi-arid, in reality the climate varies as much as the landscape. While the large inland plateau, known as the Great Karoo, is extremely hot and dry in summer, the Cape Peninsula has a Mediterranean climate, with mild, wet winters and warm to hot summers. The seasons are exactly opposite to those in the northern hemisphere – great for sun lovers seeking winter relief. With plenty of hours of sunshine, any time of year can be the right time to travel, but autumn (March–April) and spring (September–October) are particularly pleasant, when the weather's not too hot.

EXPLORING THE COUNTRY

It was, perhaps, South Africa's world-class infrastructure that clinched the bid to host the 2010 football World Cup. The country has a very good network of roads, domestic air services link most sizeable towns, while the rail network ranges from quaint local services to the luxurious Blue Train (see page 82). So, depending on time and taste, you can travel around South Africa by any combination of car, train and plane. Alternatively, you can hire a caravan, join a coach tour or even charter a helicopter. It's worth striking a balance between the cities and the countryside, and between culture and nature.

Johannesburg, a brash city built on gold, offers much in the way of shopping, eating and nightlife experiences, and the International Airport offers connecting flights to Cape Town, Durban and the Kruger National Park. Another side

FACTS AND FIGURES

Area: 1,221,000 sq km (471,430 sq miles).

Capitals: Pretoria/Tshwane (administrative), Bloemfontein (judicial) and Cape Town (legislative).

Population: 52.98 million; 22.7% speak isiZulu as mother tongue, 16% isiXhosa, 13.5% Afrikaans, 9.1% Sepedi, 9.6% English and 8% Setswana.

Provinces: KwaZulu-Natal (11 million), Gauteng (12.2 million), Eastern Cape (6.5 million), Limpopo (5.4 million), Western Cape (5.8 million), Mpumalanga (4 million), North West (3.5 million), Free State (2.7 million) and Northern Cape (1.88 million).

Government: The Republic has a constitutional democracy with a three-tier system of government. The national, provincial and local levels all have legislative and executive authority in their own spheres.

Religion: Christianity (almost 80%); Islam, Hinduism, indigenous beliefs.

of life can be experienced in the township of Soweto and, to the north west, the Sterkfontein Caves and Maropeng are highlights of the Cradle of Humankind, which is listed as a Unesco World Heritage Site thanks to its hominid fossils. North of Johannesburg is attractive Pretoria (Tshwane), South Africa's capital.

African Elephant

ECOTOURISM AND ACTIVE PURSUITS

Starved of tourism during the long years of apartheid, South Africa largely escaped the kind of environmental degradation that occurs in places with developed holiday industries. Today, conservation allows the state to guarantee the 'environmental rights' of citizens and reap the economic rewards of wildlife tourism. In fact, more wildlife roams the country today than a century ago, due to the state allowing private ownership of wildlife. And private game reserves adjoining the Kruger National Park have removed fences to allow freer movement of wild animals.

Little can beat the thrill of watching lions, rhinos, hippos and buffalo going about their daily lives in South Africa's excellent network of national parks and other game reserves.

The country's varied landscapes offer all kinds of opportunities for viewing animals in their natural habitats. In KwaZulu-Natal alone you can watch hippos cooling off in the wetlands of Greater St Lucia, or white rhinos grazing in Hluhluwe-Imfolozi Game Reserve, or bottle-nosed dolphins playing in the surf off the coast.

South Africa's sports possibilities cover a lot of ground (golf, hiking, horse riding) as well as a lot of ocean (fishing, surfing, swimming). Rugby, cricket, football, boxing and horse racing draw the big crowds. Adventure tourism opportunities include hiking trails, white-water rafting, even bungee jumping and sand-boarding (see page 89).

POLITICS AND PEOPLE

From the late 1940s, when the policy of apartheid was codified, South Africa's National Party government pursued the goal of separate development of racial groups (see page 22). This entailed the mass removal of citizens to new housing areas, a ban on interracial marriage and the segregation of schools, hotels, buses, trains and even park benches. Many petty apartheid laws were repealed in the late 1980s, while the unbanning of the anc in 1990 and simultaneous release of its most famous leader Nelson Mandela amounted to a tacit admission that the system the National government had enforced for almost half a century was both unworkable and immoral.

Almost 80 percent of South Africa's population are black and belong to a number of nations or tribes, the biggest of which are the Zulu, Xhosa, Sotho and Tswana. Roughly one in 10 of the population is white, and slightly less than 10 percent are referred to as Coloured, meaning of mixed race. Another 2.5 percent are Asian, mostly the descendants of immigrants from India. White South Africans object strongly to being considered mere settlers or immigrants in Africa, especially those whose roots go back more than three centuries to the foundation of the Dutch station at the Cape. With them the Dutch language was introduced and from it evolved Afrikaans, the mother tongue of most South African whites and Coloured people. Nearly 40 percent of whites are native English speakers, and English (an official language) is understood almost everywhere.

A BRIEF HISTORY

Much of sub-Saharan Africa came late to the pages of recorded history, but it seems that our own species, Homo sapiens, first evolved on its sunny upland plains. Long before that, more than 2.5 million years ago, a type of hominid known as *Australopithecus africanus* lived scarcely 30km (20 miles) northwest of the site where Johannesburg is now situated. Other fossils show that by 50,000 years ago a family that was recognisably human inhabited caves in Mpumalanga Province. Able to use fire and stone tools, these people were probably the ancestors of the hunter-gatherers responsible for the vivid rock paintings found all over southern Africa.

By the 5th century AD, migrating tribes from West Africa had brought an Iron-Age culture to much of what is now South Africa. When Europeans first came to Africa's southern tip they met other early inhabitants of the area—smaller, lighter-skinned

Prehistoric rock art depicts the early inhabitants of South Africa

people who hunted or herded cattle. They called the cattle-herders Hottentots and the hunters, Bushmen. Today they are classified as Khoikhoi and San; together, Khoisan.

When the first European settlers arrived in the mid-17th century, several black nations had migrated from the centre of the continent to southern Africa. There was little contact between them and the white settlers at the Cape until the mid-18th century. The Khoikhoi began to act as middle-men, but their numbers declined through war and disease until they finally faded away, blending into what has since become known as the Cape Coloured population.

THE DUTCH AT THE CAPE

Following the first sighting of the Cape of Good Hope by Portuguese explorer Bartolomeu Dias at the end of the 15th century (see page 78), the Cape became a regular port of call for European, especially Dutch, ships. Here they could take on fresh water and barter iron, beads and brandy in exchange for local cattle. Sixty Dutch crew were forced to spend almost a year at the Cape when their ship was driven ashore in 1647. Once home, their leaders recommended setting up a permanent settlement to provide facilities for ships of the Dutch East Indies Company on the way to and from Southeast Asia.

On 7 April 1652, a party of about 100 men, led by Jan van Riebeeck, landed at Table Bay and began to build a fort and prepare land for growing food. Despite clashes with the Khoikhoi,

Cape Malays

As the settlement's need for labour grew, slaves were imported in the main from the Dutch East Indies (modern Indonesia). These slaves intermarried with Khoisan, Africans and the white settlers to form a new community, known today as the Coloured people or Cape Malays.

Jan van Riebeeck at the Cape of Good Hope in the 17th century

whose grazing lands were infringed upon, the settlement was established.

The colony kept its Dutch character even after the arrival of other nationalities, notably the French Huguenots, who added expertise to the Cape wine industry. The immigrants were obliged to learn Dutch, but they brought fervour to the Calvinist tone of the colony's Dutch Reformed Church. Thus was forged a new people: the Afrikaners, or Boers (meaning farmer in Dutch). Pushing further inland, many paid little heed to the authorities in Cape Castle, still less to those in Amsterdam.

ENTER THE BRITISH

Wars in Europe sent shock waves as far as South Africa. After a French attack on the Netherlands, the British occupied the Cape colony in 1795. They returned in 1806 and again, definitively, in 1814 as a result of territory exchanges following the Napoleonic wars. The change of government shook the foundations of Cape society. Britain outlawed the slave trade in 1807, abolishing slavery throughout the Empire in 1834. Faced with a curtailed labour supply, little compensation and the imposition of the English language and legal system, many colonials began to strike out into the wilderness. The pioneers were known as the Voortrekkers (literally, 'those who pull ahead').

Much of the land they took had been abandoned shortly before as a result of Zulu raids on other tribes. The Boers forced their wagon trains deep into the heart of the subcontinent. A new British colony on the Indian Ocean coast of Natal restricted the Voortrekkers to the interior, where they established two new states: the Orange Free State between the rivers Orange and Vaal and the Transvaal Republic to the north of the Vaal.

Citing bad government and ill treatment of the black population, the British took the Transvaal in 1877. However, in 1881, following news of a British defeat at the hands of the Zulus in Natal, the Transvaalers rose against their occupiers and forced them to withdraw. The clash of British and Boer interests grated quietly until the turn of the century, when it exploded in a second, much longer and more bitter war.

Fighting between white settlers and black tribes had continued on and off since the second half of the 18th century. Frontier wars with the Xhosa, for example, were fought every 10 years or so. The struggle for usable land also underlay wars between black tribes, the most dramatic being those waged by

Fall of the Xhosa

Loss of life, land and power during the frontier wars devastated traditional Xhosa society, as they sought an explanation for these disasters. Nongqawuse, a young Xhosa prophetess, foretold that if the people killed all their cattle and destroyed all their crops, the dead would rise, new cattle would rise, and nobody would ever suffer again. Some 400,000 cattle were culled during 1856–7 and 40,000 Xhosa died as a result. They were no longer a force to be reckoned with.

The diamond rush in Kimberley left a vast gash in the earth

Zulu general Shaka, the 'black Napoleon', who died in 1828. Zulu leaders fought the Voortrekkers, then the British, and it was only in the 1880s that British firepower imposed a kind of peace.

GLITTERING HOPES

In Hopetown, on the Orange River, the first diamond was discovered in 1866. The area was invaded by fortune hunters after a giant stone of 83.5 carats appeared, and the action soon shifted north to Kimberley, where finding diamonds was almost easy. Over the next 40 years, diggers went ever deeper, until Kimberley's Big Hole had yielded 3 tons of diamonds.

Gold had been found in various parts of South Africa, but the big strike came in the Transvaal in 1886 on the highveld referred to as the Witwatersrand, or Rand, which subsequently became the site of Johannesburg. The prospector sold his claim for £10 and was never heard of again. The reef has since come up with more than 35,000 metric tons (32,000 tons) of pure gold.

Since 1881 Britain had kept her distance from events in the independent Transvaal, claiming only a vague right of veto over external alliances. However, with the Rand's riches unearthed, foreign prospectors and entrepreneurs soon flocked in.

The republic's government benefited from taxes levied on the *uitlanders* (foreigners), but denied them a voice in running the country. Cecil Rhodes, the mining magnate and prime minister of Cape Colony, plotted an uprising of the Transvaal *uitlanders*, but his accomplice, Dr Jameson, jumped the gun, leading an invading party from Rhodesia, which was quickly overcome by the better armed Boers. Three years later, in 1899, the British and the Afrikaners openly fought out the issue.

THE ANGLO-BOER WAR

The Afrikaners were led at this time by the long-established president of the Transvaal—the bearded, top-hatted Paul

Public library and statue of Queen Victoria, Port Elizabeth

Kruger. Three of his prominent military chiefs, Louis Botha, Jan Smuts and J.B.M. Hertzog, were destined to become prime ministers of the Union of South Africa. Although initially outnumbered by a ratio of five to one, the Boers held their own through innovative commando tactics.

British strategist Lord Kitchener employed harsh methods. Families of Boer soldiers were held in concentration camps. Some 26,000 inmates died, mostly of disease. Less publicised were the conditions in separate camps built for blacks, where the death toll was over 13,000. The revelations shocked British opinion and strengthened the inward-looking Afrikaners.

After two and a half years of fighting, the Boers conceded defeat in May 1902. Shortly after, Britain agreed to the formation of a self-governing dominion. They nevertheless managed to alienate the Afrikaners and did not attempt to extend the limited rights of non-whites that existed in the Cape and Natal.

The Union of South Africa, created in 1910, was an amalgam of the Transvaal and Orange Free State with the Cape and Natal, Britain's two colonies. So delicate were regional sensibilities that power bases were spread around the country, with Pretoria the administrative capital, Bloemfontein the judicial capital and Cape Town the seat of Parliament. Foreshadowing future policies it was decided that only whites could be elected as members of parliament.

THE WORLD WARS AND AFTERMATH

Only four years after creating the Union of South Africa the British Empire went to war with Germany. South African troops were quick to seize the German colony of South West Africa (present-day Namibia) and played a major part in the long campaign against German-led forces in East Africa.

By the time World War II broke out, Jan Smuts was in his second term as prime minister. Beating a strong parliamentary minority in favour of neutrality, he led his country into the war against Nazi Germany. South African troops entered the fray in North Africa and Italy.

Although Smuts drafted the human rights declaration of the United Nations charter, South Africa was almost immediately under fire for its own human rights record and ended up pulling out of the UN agencies. Under pressure from the

APARTHEID

Arguably, the path of racial segregation can be traced back to the use of slave labour by white settlers in the 1650s. It was, however, in the 1950s that the systematic separation of the races was taken to its extreme. The concept of 'separateness' and white superiority was implemented in law by the National Party. They enacted a Population Registration Act in 1950 to slot all citizens into an appropriate race group, and to outlaw interracial marriage and sexual relations. The Group Areas Act divided every town into defined sectors where only members of particular groups could own or occupy property, requiring the removal of many Coloured and Asian households. Dr Hendrick Verwoerd, a chief promoter of apartheid legislation and prime minister from 1958, consolidated a policy to convert African reserves into 'independent homelands', another way to deprive citizens of access to political rights.

Most resented of all were the 'pass laws', which restricted the movement of the African population. It is no surprise that the 1950s also saw a rise in resistance. While confrontations between campaigners and the authorities were initially non-violent, the tone was set to change following the massacre at Sharpeville and the subsequent banning of the ANC and PAC.

multi-racial Commonwealth, South Africa withdrew from its relationship with Britain, becoming an independent republic in 1961. Western nations imposed trade embargos, especially on military equipment.

Hector Pietersen, first victim of the riot police in Soweto, 1976

SOCIETY UNDER TENSION

In 1948, the all-white electorate voted out Smuts' United Party in favour of the National Party, whose segregationist policy of apartheid (see box) made South Africa an international pariah.

Violent protests against apartheid, and the government's reactions, kept South Africa in the international spotlight. In 1960, opposition to the pass laws culminated in a demonstration at Sharpeville, in the Transvaal, when the police opened fire, killing 69 black people. In 1976, after the government enforced the use of Afrikaans in schools, protests erupted in Soweto and spread to townships across the country. Over 600 were killed during this period of resistance and the government placed a ban on individuals and organisations suspected of subversion.

New unrest sweeping the townships during the mid-1980s prompted a state of emergency. Thousands, almost all blacks, were arrested and then held without trial. Violence dominated television screens abroad until news crews were finally barred.

Under growing internal and external pressures the government decided to scrap much of the legal structure of apartheid.

Nelson Mandela statue, Sandton City

In 1990 President F.W. de Klerk legalised the African National Congress and other banned organisations, and released ANC leader Nelson Mandela after 27 historic years in prison.

MIRACLE OF DEMOCRACY

The country's first all-inclusive election, held in April 1994, was relayed round the world as a 'miracle of democracy'. Nelson Mandela came to power as president at the head of the ANC, in a government of national unity. At last South Africa had a democratic constitution, allowing all its citizens to study, work and move freely in their own country.

On the whole, South Africa's first dozen years of democratic rule can be adjudged a success story. The country has enjoyed high levels of political stability and social freedom. The ANC government, voted back into power under Thabo Mbeki in 1999 and 2004, has done much to address housing shortages, and sub-standard educational and health facilities. However, the country still faces many problems, notably the high rate of violent crime, a spiralling Aids pandemic, economic uncertainty, high unemployment (nearly 23 percent in 2015), social inequality and rampant corruption, epitomised by the court cases surrounding ANC party chief and the country's president, Jacob Zuma.

Despite these problems, South Africa is very much the continent's superpower and the overall picture is one of hope, enthusiasm and energy.

HISTORICAL LANDMARKS

c.8000BC San inhabit the southwestern regions of southern Africa.

From 200AD The semi-nomadic Khoikhoi begin farming the land.

1488 Bartolomeu Dias lands at Mossel Bay and sails round the Cape.

1652 Jan van Riebeeck sets up Dutch supply station at Table Bay.

1820–8 Zulu king Shaka extends his territory.

1879 British and Zulu forces clash; Zulus decisively defeated.

1880–1 The Transvaal declares itself a republic. First Anglo-Boer war.

1886 Gold discovered in the Transvaal; Johannesburg founded.

1899–1902 Second Anglo-Boer War, in which Boers are beaten.

1910 The Union of South Africa is established.

1913 Natives Land Act is passed, limiting land ownership for blacks.

1948 National Party under D.F. Malan elected; apartheid acts follow.

1952 The ANC launches the Defiance Campaign.

1961 South Africa becomes a republic and leaves the Commonwealth.

1964 Following his arrest in 1962, Mandela is given a life sentence.

1976 Police violence in Soweto ignites resistance across country.

1984 Archbishop Desmond Tutu is awarded Nobel Peace Prize.

1990 Process to end apartheid begins; Nelson Mandela released.

1994 Nelson Mandela is elected first black president.

2009 Jacob Zuma is sworn in as national president.

2010 South Africa hosts the FIFA World Cup.

2013 Nelson Mandela dies aged 95. Ten days of national mourning follow his death.

2014 Jacob Zuma re-elected; Paralympic athlete Oscar Pistorius convicted of culpable homicide after fatally shooting his girlfriend, Reeva Steenkamp.

2015 Allegations arise suggesting the South African government offered bribes to FIFA members to secure the World Cup in 2010. Pistorius' charge of culpable homicide is replaced by a murder charge. Further sentencing postponed until 2016.

2016 High Court rules that President Zuma must repay part of the $23m of public funds spent on the renovation of his house in 2009. Pistorius sentenced to a further six years imprisonment.

WHERE TO GO

The size of France, Germany, Holland and Belgium combined, South Africa is too big to get to know in a single visit, so in the following pages we set out the highlights to help you choose an itinerary.

We begin in dynamic Johannesburg, which is situated in the province of Gauteng. After a look at nearby Pretoria (Tshwane), with a diversion to the resort of Sun City, we head for Mpumalanga Province and South Africa's prime tourist attraction, the Kruger National Park. Crossing the mountains of KwaZulu-Natal, we come to bustling Durban on the Indian Ocean and take a trip north into Zululand. Then we jump to Port Elizabeth, following the coast clockwise along the Garden Route and all the way to Cape Town, which becomes a base for visits to the Cape of Good Hope and to the Cape wine country. Finally, the circle is completed by looking at various ways back to Johannesburg: the luxurious Blue Train; the long drive across the Great Karoo to Kimberley; or still further north to the fringes of the Kalahari Desert.

GAUTENG

Gauteng is a province that accounts for just 1.5 percent of South Africa's surface area, yet its estimated 12 million residents represent a quarter of the national population and generate 35 percent of its GDP. The explanation for this unusual concentration of wealth and populace is simple – gold.

Most of the world's great cities were built on a river, but Johannesburg – Gauteng's bustling administrative capital – owes its existence to an underground stream of gold. The discovery of this rich seam in 1886 transformed the meagre

Clifton Beach, Cape Town

grazing land above it into South Africa's biggest city in just three years.

JOHANNESBURG

As southern Africa's transport hub, **Johannesburg ❶** (known as Jo'burg or Jozi) is often considered to be merely a spring-board for travel to other parts of South Africa or the conti-nent. Nevertheless, it offers some of Africa's best nightlife, shops and hotels. The city is at its best in summer (Nov–Mar); warm, sunny mornings may turn into stormy afternoons, but torrential rains soon move on, leaving the city refreshed.

Like every South African city, Johannesburg's population patterns remain influenced by the racial segregation laws enacted under apartheid. Some 50,000 Asians were resettled in their own suburb, Lenasia, and blacks were assigned to vast townships on the outskirts, such as Soweto and Alexandria.

The skyline of Johannesburg

CITY CENTRE

Downtown Johannesburg is a colourful mix of tall skyscrapers, small Indian bazaars and traditional African *muti* (medicine) shops, where smart-suited office workers rub shoulders with beggars and hawkers. It is also a noted crime hotspot, so don't wander around with an expensive camera, watch or pair of sunglasses, or more money than you actually need.

Street vendors outside the Market Theatre, Johannesburg

Throughout the city centre a relaxation of restrictions on street trading has resulted in hundreds of hawkers setting up market stalls or simply spreading a cloth on the ground and selling every imaginable commodity. Africa has come to South Africa's financial hub.

Among all the office buildings it's hard to find many historical monuments, but local preservationists are proud of the red-brick **Rissik Street Post Office**, which was started in 1897 and adorned with a clock tower after the Anglo–Boer War.

Over in Bree Street is the Newtown Cultural Precinct, a former fruit and vegetable market. Here you will find the **MuseuMAfricA** (Tue–Sun 9am–5pm; free), with an excellent range of African historical and cultural exhibits. The other end of the long building houses the **Market Theatre** complex (www.markettheatre.co.za), which nurtured a thriving protest theatre movement in the apartheid era.

To the west of the Newtown market, a big concrete shopping centre in vaguely Moghul style called **Oriental Plaza**

Nelson Mandela Square, Sandton City

(www.orientalplaza.co.za) stretches from Bree Street to Main Street. The smell of spices greets you before you arrive. Connecting courtyards are ringed by Indian restaurants, snack bars and shops.

Housed in a building designed by Sir Edwin Lutyens, the **Johannesburg Art Gallery** (http://friendsofjag.org; Tue–Sun 10am–5pm; free; guided tours available) is set in **Joubert Park**, the city's oldest park. The collection concentrates on the 19th and early 20th centuries, and includes a small but representative display of South African art. Bear in mind that the surrounding area, despite recent improvements, remains one of the worst spots for street crime in the city.

Immediately northwest of the city centre, in Braamfontein, the **University of the Witwatersrand** (www.wits.ac.za) is Africa's biggest English-language university. To the west of Wits is the modern campus of Rand Afrikaans University.

The **Origins Centre** (www.origins.org.za), situated on the Wits University campus, traces the origins of humankind in Africa with a focus on rock art created by the San and found at various sites around the country. A centrepiece of the museum is what is thought to be the earliest image made by man.

Further east lies **Constitution Hill** (www.constitution hill.org.za), a former prison where Nelson Mandela and Mahatma Ghandi were once held, which is now home to the Women's Gaol Museum, Number Four Museum, Old Fort Museum and the Constitutional Court. The three museums collectively tell the grim story of South Africa's long struggle for human rights. Tours of the Constitutional Court are available, where you can witness a real court hearing from the visitor decks. The court building also houses a fine collection of works by eminent South African artists.

Going for gold

Johannesburg grew from the diggers' camps that proliferated following the discovery of gold in 1886. Since that time, the gold mining industry has been the backbone of South Africa's economy. Miners face tough working conditions – even though refrigerated air is constantly pumped through the networks of narrow shafts, air temperatures often exceed 32°C (90°F).

North of the city centre, the modest but pleasant **Johannesburg Zoo** (www.jhbzoo.org.za; daily 8.30am–5.30pm) lies in Rosebank, also known for its shopping malls and occasional art displays at Zoo Lake on Sundays. The nearby suburbs of Norwood and Melville are good for eating out and, further north, fashionable **Sandton** is South Africa's financial centre and has excellent hotels, a vast shopping complex and the open-air **Nelson Mandela Square** (www.nelsonmandela square.co.za).

SOWETO

An organised day tour of **Soweto** (a contraction of South Western Townships) can be arranged through any hotel and

Maropeng Visitor Centre

makes a striking contrast to hanging out in the prosperous northern suburbs. Tours pass through various neighbourhoods, most poor and cramped, except the exclusive street known as Millionaires' Row.

The site of No. 14 Shaft of Crown Mines in Alamein Rd, southwest of the city centre, is the focus of **Gold Reef City** (www.tsogosun.com/gold-reef-city-casino/theme-park), a theme park with rides, shows, bars and hotel, all in the style of the 1890s, as well as restaurants and shops. The highlight is a trip through an authentic gold mine. Wearing protective gear and miners' lamps, visitors descend 220m (722ft) below ground.

Next to the Gold Reef complex is the **Museum of Apartheid** (www.apartheidmuseum.org; daily 9am–5pm; unsuitable for young children), with graphic displays illustrating the grim history of apartheid and the perils of racial discrimination. If you are interested in history, you should also visit the **Mandela House** (www.nelsonmandelamuseum.org.za), the **Hector Pieterson Museum**, which is dedicated to the Soweto student uprising, and the **Satyagraha House** (www.satyagraha house.com), the former residence of Mohandas Gandhi, now an engaging museum.

Part of the 'Cradle of Humankind' Unesco World Heritage Site, the **Sterkfontein Caves** ❷ (www.maropeng.co.za; Tue–Sun 9am–5pm), west of Johannesburg, have yielded more than 500 hominid fossils, most famously a 2.5 million-year-old skull discovered in 1936 and nicknamed 'Mrs Ples' (short for *Plesianthropus transvaalensis*, though the skull is now assigned to the species *Australopithecus Africanus*, and thought to be male). A visit is best combined with a two-hour guided tour of nearby **Maropeng Visitor Centre** (www.maropeng.co.za; Tue–Sun 9am–5pm), also part of the Cradle of Humankind.

PRETORIA (TSHWANE)

In the spring (October and November) the garden city of **Pretoria** ❸ shimmers in a purple bloom of 60,000 jacaranda trees, originally introduced to South Africa from Brazil. You'll find Pretoria an agreeable place at any time, though, with beautiful parks and some innovative architecture.

The city of Tshwane, which is the recently adopted name for the Greater Pretoria metropolitan area, has a population of almost 3 million. Although Pretoria remains a joint capital of the new South Africa, the government and civil service is no longer dominated by whites, and the city has largely shed its negative image as the apartheid administration's heartland.

Pretoria's historic heart is **Church Square**, where early settlers built their first church in the 1850s. A statue of Paul Kruger – the craggy patriarch who was elected president of the Transvaal Republic four times in the late 19th century – stands in the middle of the square.

Some distinguished official buildings from earlier days face the square: the old **Raadsaal** (parliament), in Italian Renaissance

Pretoria's Union Buildings

style; the old **South African Reserve Bank**, designed by Sir Herbert Baker; and the **Palace of Justice**, used as a hospital during the British occupation of 1900. Among the modern buildings near the square that lift the skyline is the **Volkskas Centre**, headquarters of the first Afrikaner-controlled bank.

Strijdom Square, located just down the street from the Volkskas skyscraper, is home to a vibrant market. At the time of writing, the surrounding area is a construction site as the old municipal building, the Munitoria, which was demolished in 2013, is in the process of being replaced by the Tshwane House (due to open in 2017). Adjoining the square is the **State Theatre complex**, which comprises six auditoria (www.statetheatre.co.za).

If you really can't manage a trip to a game park, you might look in at Pretoria's **National Zoological Gardens** (www.nzg.ac.za; daily 8.30am–5.30pm, last entry at 4.30pm), with more than 3,500 species from around the world; a cable car is suspended above some areas. The **National Cultural History Museum** (daily 8am–4pm), located in the Old Mint building on Visagie Street, explores South Africa's diverse cultures from early San rock art to the present day, with a vast collection of exhibits. Sir Herbert Baker designed Pretoria's noblest architectural ensemble, the **Union Buildings**, a couple of mirror-image structures linked by a semi-circular colonnade. This big ministerial complex, the site of President Mandela's inauguration in 1994, looks down on formal gardens (daily; free) of brilliant flowers, sculpted trees and flawless lawns.

Bird-watchers don't know which way to turn in South Africa, where even suburban gardens harbour the most exotic birds in wild colour schemes. For a rapid initiation try the **Transvaal Museum** (www.ditsong.org.za; daily 8am–4pm, last admission 3pm) in Paul Kruger Street, where every species of South African bird is identified.

SOUTH OF PRETORIA

To the south of the city in the Fountains Valley Nature Reserve, a military stronghold built in 1898, commands strategic views of both Pretoria and the fertile countryside around. **Fort**

SUN CITY

South Africa's answer to Las Vegas lies 90 minutes' drive west of Johannesburg, on the fringes of the Kalahari. During the late 1970s, the austere restrictions in South Africa encouraged businessman Sol Kerzner to create an escape valve in what was then the homeland of Bophuthatswana. Today, Sun City is part of the North West Province of South Africa and the resort's hedonistic pleasures are geared towards the family as much as the gambler.

Rising like a mirage from the dusty bushveld, this glitzy resort contains casinos, cinemas, restaurants and numerous hotels. The extraordinary Lost City complex is the biggest such project ever achieved in Africa and features a spectacular five-star hotel (see page 133), complete with artificial beach and wave pool. Outdoor facilities include a world-class golf course and an artificial lake for waterskiing and parasailing. Nearby is Pilanesberg National Park (see page 37).

Buses run frequently to Sun City from the Rotunda at Johannesburg's railway station and many tour companies operate excursions for a day or longer. For resort details visit www.suninternational.com.

Klapperkop (Tue–Sun 10am–5pm) has been spruced up and now serves as a museum of the military history of the Zuid-Afri-kaansche Republiek, the Transvaal republic of the 19th century.

For miles around Pretoria, the hilltop **Voortrekker Monument** (www.vtm.org.za; daily May–Aug 8am–5pm, Sep–Apr until 6pm) stands out. The looming structure was built as a shrine to the fortitude of the pioneers of the 1830s who trekked from the Cape to the Transvaal to perpetuate their language, religion and way of life.

Inside the granite monument a sculpted frieze commemorates incidents that took place during the treks. The monument's museum houses the Voortrekker Tapestry, a series of vivid needlework panels depicting events of the Great Trek.

FURTHER AFIELD

Forty kilometres (25 miles) east of Pretoria, at **Cullinan**, is the Premier Diamond Mine (www.diamondtourscullinan.co.za; surface tours Mon–Fri 10.30am and 2pm, Sat–Sun 10.30am and noon, no under-10s; underground tours on request, no under-16s), a historic site in its own right: the 3,106-carat Cullinan diamond was unearthed here in 1905. From the fist-sized stone were hewn the Star of Africa and other gems now among the British Crown Jewels. The mine is still in business, producing about a million carats a year, though most of the stones are used for industrial purposes. Tour operators in Johannesburg and Pretoria run excursions to the mine, or you can go by car. You'll need strong shoes.

Ndebele people

Well known for their colourful geometric wallpaintings, the Ndebele people derive from the Nguni of KwaZulu-Natal. Those found to the north of Pretoria are the southern Ndebele, whose homeland of KwaNdebele was established in 1984. Ndebele people are also found in Zimbabwe.

The **Hartbeespoort Dam**, 35km (22 miles) west of Pretoria, in a beautiful location against the backdrop of the Magaliesberg Mountains, is the setting for numerous small holiday resorts, as well as a good snake park. The **Ann Van Dyk Cheetah Centre**, off the R513 near the dam (www.dewildt.co.za; tours only; Tue, Thu, Sat and Sun at 8am booking essential, Mon, Wed, Fri 8.30–11.30am and daily 1.30–4.30pm; no children under six; family tours daily 9.30am and 2.30pm) is the first place where the cheetah was successfully bred in captivity.

African elephant on Madikwe Game Reserve

Situated 40km (25 miles) northwest of Pretoria, the **Tswaing Crater Museum** (www.ditsong.org.za; daily 7.30am–4pm) protects a 1.4-km (nearly 1-mile) wide meteorite crater and the brackish lake on its floor. The hike to the crater takes around 2½–3 hours.

Two hours' drive northwest of Pretoria, the 500 sq km (195 sq mile) **Pilanesberg National Park** ❹ (www.pilanesberg-game-reserve.co.za) consists of a scenic collapsed caldera where lion, elephant and rhino roam freely alongside various antelope and 350 bird species. Good internal roads and a wide range of accommodation options from campsites to the luxury Sun City complex make Pilanesberg ideal for a short self-drive safari out of Gauteng.

A striking view of the Blyde River Canyon in Mpumalanga

A more exclusive game-viewing experience is offered at **Madikwe Game Reserve** (www.madikwe-game-reserve.co.za; access to overnight visitors only) on the Great Marico River on the Botswana border, where a similar range of species can be seen on guided game drives out of a few small and relatively costly lodges. Like the Pilanesberg, Madikwe has one definite advantage over the Kruger Park and environs, namely that it is free of malaria.

MPUMALANGA AND LIMPOPO

The mountain region east of Gauteng is one of South Africa's favourite holiday retreats, particularly as a stopover en route to or from the splendid game reserves of the north.

From Pretoria or Johannesburg to the Kruger National Park is about 400km (248 miles) on excellent roads. The trip eastwards starts in the grassy plains of the highveld but, less than halfway, the scenery dramatically changes. One minute you could be in Scotland, the next the hills are as rugged as those in North Dakota, then suddenly the road plunges from cool spruce forests to banana plantations on the hot, humid lowveld.

ON THE ROAD TO KRUGER

If you're in a hurry, you can fly to the Kruger National Park or one of the private reserves. Travellers less worried about time can drive or take coach tours, going out and back on Route N4. If you have a day or two to spare, though, it's more interesting to take one route to Kruger, travel through the park, leave by another gate and return to Gauteng on a different road, taking in some of the following highlights of Mpumalanga and Limpopo provinces.

Nelspruit (Mbombela), on the N4 and the Crocodile River, is the centre of a rich fruit-growing area which is surrounded by orange groves as well as orchards of mangoes, avocados and lichees. The town itself is handsome, with a population of more than 58,000 and a contemporary stadium with roof support columns resembling giraffes, which was specially built for the FIFA World Cup in 2010.

An alternative route to the Kruger Park goes through the town of **Lydenburg** (Mashishing), where a few early buildings survive from the 1850s, and over **Long Tom Pass** to **Sabie**, the site of a rich seam of gold, long since exhausted, and a brewery. Long Tom Pass is named after a gun used by the Boers against the British in 1900; the scenery is striking for its scale and emptiness. The local pine forests are popular among the mountain bikers.

Pilgrim's Rest, in a valley to the north, is well worth a diversion. Amid delightful pastoral scenery the heavily gouged hillsides give a clue to the past. A prospector named Alec 'Wheelbarrow' Patterson first panned gold here in 1873. News of the easy pickings spread quickly and Pilgrim's Rest took on all the trappings of a gold rush – 18 pubs could hardly cope with the crowds of miners. In the 20th century, as the mining

A view from the bridge at Bourke's Luck Potholes

technology became more and more sophisticated, the gold effectively ran out in 1972. When operations were closed down the provincial authorities bought up the town and preserved it as an oasis of nostalgia, with museums, gold-panning demonstrations, shops and hotels (www.pilgrimsrest.org.za).

The forestry centre of nearby **Graskop** is a small town with mini-markets where you can replenish your picnic supplies. Past the regional centre of **Hazyview**, the road leads to the Paul Kruger Gate of the Kruger National Park.

THE PANORAMA ROUTE

If you can take a little more time, try to work out a route that allows you to see the **Blyde River Canyon** ❺. 'Awe-inspiring' is no exaggeration for the views in this part of the world, where the Drakensberg Mountains mark the transition from highveld to low. The geological surprises of the escarpment include rock faces weirdly coloured by minerals, lichens and algae. The gorge itself is visible from many lookout points that are reached by long or short walks from the road. Three sandstone peaks–round outcrops topped by grass-covered cupolas–are called the **Three Rondavels**. Beyond them, **Mariepskop** is a mountain that has been squared off like an aircraft carrier. Hillsides plunge to the river as it zigzags through the creases, widening at last behind the Blyde River Dam.

Visitors to **God's Window** are rewarded by a panoramic view of the lowveld. Near Bourke's Luck, named after an old gold mine, the rivers Blyde ('joyful') and Treur ('sorrowful') converge in a three-way gorge. Three aluminium bridges offer views of this natural drama, from thundering waterfalls to **Bourke's Luck Potholes**, which seem to have been excavated by some gigantic ice-cream scoop. Displays at a visitor centre explain the local natural history. Accommodation is available at the **Forever Blyde Canyon Resort** (www.foreverblyde canyon.co.za; tel: 086-122 6966).

KRUGER NATIONAL PARK

Close to 2 million hectares in size, the **Kruger National Park** ❻ (www.sanparks.org/parks/kruger; park gates open Nov–Feb 5.30am–6.30pm, Oct and Mar 5.30am–6pm, Apr and Aug–Sep 6am–6pm, May–Jul 6am–5.30pm; advance booking advisable) is South Africa's biggest wildlife sanctuary. It contains more mammal species than any other game reserve in Africa, with the exception of Kafue National Park in Zambia. At least 13,750 elephants live within its boundaries, together with an estimated 37,130 buffalo, between 132,000 and 176,000 impala and 35,000 zebra. Close to half a million people visit each year.

Take your pills

Before arriving in the area, don't forget to start taking anti-malaria pills, since both the Kruger Park and the private reserves alongside it are in a malaria zone (see page 121).

In recent years, most of the non-hunting reserves in the eastern lowveld have removed their fences bordering the Kruger National Park, so that wildlife can move freely between. The Kruger Park now also forms the core of the Great Limpopo Transfrontier Park, which – following full amalgamation with Zimbabwe's Gonarezhou National Park and Mozambique's Limpopo National Park – will probably rank as Africa's largest game reserve with an area of 35,000 sq km (22,000 sq miles).

Predicting the weather for this vast park is tricky, but the rainy season extends from September or October to March or April – mostly as brief thunder showers.

ACCOMMODATION

A place to stay may be reserved up to a year in advance through a travel agency or by writing to the SANParks, PO Box 787, Pretoria 0001. If you leave it to the last minute, you still stand a chance if you call the reservation service (tel: 012-428 9111). You can also use SANParks website for information and bookings at www.sanparks.org.

If no space is available, you might consider joining a package tour, as the tour operators make block bookings; or you could try to find accommodation in a hotel or camping ground outside the park but near enough for you to go in for day trips.

There are 18 rest camps, mostly in the park's southern half, where visitor traffic is concentrated. Those listed below have a restaurant, shop, petrol station and varied accommodation:

Berg-en-dal (www.bergendalcamp.com). An upmarket, modern camp set in hilly landscape overlooking the Matjulu Dam. Its well-fenced grounds are one of the few places where you can walk in the park.

Lower Sabie (www.lowersabierestcamp.com). A relatively small camp set attractively on the banks of a dam on the Sabie River in a prime viewing area.

Olifants (www.sanparks.org/parks/kruger/camps/olifants). As the name suggests, this camp is in elephant country, set on a clifftop above the Olifants River, haunt of hippos. The surrounding roads offer reliable game viewing.

Shingwedzi (www.sanparks.org/parks/kruger/camps/shingwedzi). A rustic camp, set attractively on the stretch of the eponymous river above the Kanniedood Dam.

A leopard at Kruger National Park

Skukuza (www.sanparks.org/parks/kruger/camps/skukuza). More beds than any other camp and also more facilities, including a bank, post office and a car hire agency. It also lies at

A rhino at Kruger National Park

the heart of some of the best game-viewing roads.

ON THE LOOKOUT

Unless you pay attention you could spend hours roaming the park and see nothing more glamorous than antelope. Keep your eyes shifting from near to far, peering into the shadows, alert for any movement or discrepancy. Pay special attention to waterholes and rivers, as the largest concentrations of animals are seen in these places. Remember it's best to drive at well below the 50km/h (31mph) limit – especially on dirt roads, where there is more dust to stir up (see page 117).

In the African summer the best times for spotting game are from sunrise to perhaps 11am and again in the late afternoon in the hour before the park and camp gates close. In the cooler season the waterholes are active from predawn to noon and game can be seen at any time of day, though predators remain most active in the early morning and late afternoon.

WILDERNESS TRAILS

Perhaps the irony has struck you: in game parks it's the humans who are confined–to camps and cars. In the Kruger, the way to escape this restriction is to join a Wilderness Trail group–eight hardy trekkers accompanied by an armed tracker and ranger. The trail followers, travelling on foot, stay out in the bush for three nights. Only small numbers of visitors (aged 12 to 65) can be accepted. Reservations can be made one year in advance, or you can always try for a last-minute cancellation (tel: 0 12 428 9111).

THE RESIDENTS OF KRUGER PARK

Antelope. A generic term for ungulates from the wildebeest to the tiny steenbok. Of the 21 species here, the most common are impala.

Baboon. A troop of baboons is held in line by the big, dominant males, who grow to weigh nearly 41kg (90lbs) and can live to the age of 45.

Birds. Of the park's 505 species, several are rare outside of protected areas, including the saddle-billed stork and kori bustard.

Buffalo. Africa's only species of wild cattle, these heavily built animals stay close to waterholes or rivers, and tend to be more active at night.

Cheetah. This sleek spotted cat hunts its prey in broad daylight, reaching speeds of more than 100km/h (62mph) in short bursts.

Elephant. The largest land mammal, the African elephant can weigh as much as 6,300kg (6 tons). Females roam in loose-knit herds; males leave around age 12, drifting between herds or forming bachelor groups.

Giraffe. The world's tallest animal, male giraffes can grow to 5.5m (18ft). Vulnerable to attack by lions, they sleep briefly, standing up.

Hippopotamus. Weighing up to 2,000kg (2 tons), hippos lack sweat glands and submerge themselves by day to keep cool, grazing at dusk.

Spotted hyena. This alleged scavenger is also an efficient hunter. Clans of 10–100, led by a dominant female, are active mainly at night.

Leopard. A secretive nocturnal hunter, the leopard is hard to spot. It can usually be found along rivers, among rocky outcrops, behind foliage, or up trees, where it will often haul its kill to dine in comparative safety.

Lion. Lionesses do most of the hunting, but a hungry male will drive off the rest of the group at feeding time.

Rhinoceros. Poaching for horns has all but wiped out South African rhino herds. Kruger Park is one of the last major strongholds of this endangered species. There are two kinds of rhino: the square-lipped, or 'white', and the hook-lipped, or 'black', which is the more aggressive.

Zebra. Numbering about 30,000 in the Kruger Park, this timid creature feeds on grass alone, migrating often in search of new fields.

PRIVATE GAME PARKS

Another way to get close to nature – more comfortable but more expensive – is to book in at a **private game park**. Several of these operate in the bushveld along the western border of Kruger Park. Two- to five-day packages are offered, which include flights from Johannesburg to the airstrips at Phalaborwa or Skukuza (or to one of the reserves that has its own strip).

In a private reserve, transport is by open Land Rover, with expert rangers and trackers as guides. Vehicles are linked by radio, so word can be spread when rare animals are sighted. You can do more successful spotting in the hours around dawn and dusk than you can in the national parks, and night safaris with spotlights reveal the nocturnal creatures you might never otherwise see. By day, rangers and trackers lead walks, while teaching you some of the secrets of the bush.

Luxury lodges, such as **MalaMala** (www.malamala.com), **Sabi Sabi** (www.sabisabi.com) and **Londolozi** (www.londolozi. com; see page 134), cosset their guests with the most attentive service and haute cuisine. Several other private establishments are somewhat less expensive but nevertheless provide expert

Lions are the largest of Africa's three big cats

rangers, air-conditioned accommodation, good food and swimming pools. Among a dozen or so in this group are **Thornybush** (www.thorny bush.co.za) and **Inyati** (www. inyati.co.za). Information on accommodation in the private reserves, as well as in the national parks, is given in a brochure published by South African Tourism (see pages 111 and 127).

Hiking in Royal Natal National Park

KWAZULU-NATAL

KwaZulu-Natal province makes up only 8 percent of the nation's territory, but therein lies a remarkable geographical diversity, ranging from snow-prone mountains to a selection of beaches on the warm Indian Ocean. The people, too, range from Anglo to Zulu. Vasco da Gama, the Portuguese navigator, first sighted these shores on Christmas Day in 1497 – hence the province's original name, 'Natal', Portuguese for Christmas. Following the political changes of April 1994 the province was renamed KwaZulu-Natal. Its capital is Pieter-maritzburg, but its largest city is the Port of Durban.

UKHAHLAMBA-DRAKENSBERG PARK

The provincial conservation authority, KZN Wildlife (www.kznwildlife.com), is responsible for about 60 reserves and parks, providing comfortable cottages and chalets and plenty of attractive campgrounds. Some of the most impressive reserves are in the uKhahlamba-Drakensberg in the west along the frontier with the Kingdom of Lesotho. Stone Age Bushmen were attracted here because of the availability of small game and fresh water. They were driven out by a succession of tribes, most recently the Ngwaneni, who today live within sight of the uKhahlamba-Drakensberg peaks in their traditional wattle huts, shaped like haystacks.

Proclaimed a Unesco World Heritage Site in 2000, the KwaZulu-Natal part of this vast mountain range has long been protected within a series of conservation areas, most famously the Royal Natal National Park, the Giant's Castle Game Reserve, and the Kamberg and Loteni Nature Reserves. Extending over a total area of 243,000 hectares (600,453 acres), these contiguous protected areas are now collectively referred to as the **uKhahlamba-Drakensberg Park ❼**, a combination of the Zulu and Afrikaans names for the spine-like range, which translate respectively as 'Barrier Of Spears' and 'Dragon's Mountains'.

A geological phenomenon known as the **Amphitheatre** constitutes the climax to the **Royal Natal National Park**. The panorama looks as if Mount Rushmore had been placed atop alpine foothills; the cliffs shoot down to steep green slopes. For mountain climbers, the highest peak in this part of the range, Mont-Aux-Sources, is a two-day undertaking: 3,282m (10,765ft) above sea level and 45km (28 miles) of difficult climbing, with stupendous views as a reward. Mont-Aux-Sources is also accessible from the Free State via Qwa Qwa.

The inhabitants of Royal Natal National Park include several species of mountain antelope, as well as large colonies of baboons and dassies (rock-climbing mammals that look like oversized guinea pigs). Bird-watchers have counted nearly 200 species. For nature-lovers of all kinds there are hiking trails and easy walks through enthralling scenery.

The **Giant's Castle Game Reserve**, another Drakensberg wilderness, contains fantastic rock formations, along with caves and various treasures of Bushman rock art. The 'castle' itself, a few feet higher than Mont-Aux-Sources, is so awe-inspiring that the Africans called it 'The Mountain Not To Point At'. Wildlife includes eland (the biggest antelope) and a giant vulture, the lammergeyer. Storm clouds gather in these mountains on most summer afternoons.

How it falls in Howick

It's all downhill, slowly, from Giant's Castle to the coast. About halfway, at a refreshing altitude of 1,000m (3,280ft), is the resort centre of **Howick**. On the edge of town, the **Howick Falls**, plunging from street level into an abyss in the Umgeni Valley Nature Reserve, is a national monument.

PIETERMARITZBURG

Some 24km (15 miles) southeast of Howick is **Pietermaritzburg**, the provincial capital, which is named after two Voortrekker leaders, Piet Retief and Gerrit Maritz. The name is routinely shortened to Maritzburg. A city of parks and gardens with a population of about 600,000, it's at its best in spring when the azaleas are in bloom.

The founders of 1838 built wide streets and Cape Dutch houses, but their dreams of an unfettered Boer culture soon came to an end; the British occupied the town in 1842. Pioneer mementos, such as rifles, kitchen implements and

Pietermaritzburg City Hall

a case full of *kappies* (bonnets), are displayed in the **Voortrekker Complex** of the **Msunduzi Museum** (www.msunduzimuseum.org.za; Mon–Fri 9am–4pm, Sat 9am–1pm). A low building in Cape style, which dates from the year 1840, it began its existence as the Church of the Vow, built after the Battle of Blood River. Next door is the restored home of the Voortrekker hero, Andries Pretorius. Many claim that the fine Victorian **City Hall**, built in 1902, is the largest all-brick building south of the equator. Little shops and law offices line the narrow alleys nearby, whose names–like Chancery Lane and Gray's Inn Lane – evoke London's Inns of Court. This area was the financial district, too, until the local stock exchange went out of business in the depression of 1931

The N3 from Pietermaritzburg to Durban, one of South Africa's best highways, passes through subtropical countryside that becomes ever more lush towards the coast. About halfway to the coast the motorway skirts the spectacular **Valley of a Thousand Hills**, through which the short but powerful Umgeni River journeys to the Indian Ocean.

This is Zulu country and **Phezulu Safari Park** (www.phezulu safaripark.co.za; daily 8am–4.30pm; coach parties from Durban) is one of the main attractions. Each 'beehive' hut in this living museum illustrates an aspect of tribal life. A highlight is the dancing display to the rhythm of a drum and two-toned string instruments.

DURBAN

They come from all parts of South Africa to hit the beaches and ride the surf or the roller coaster at **Durban** ➑ and, somehow, the town succeeds in combining the roles of brash beach resort and the busiest port in Africa.

Durban has come a long way since 1824, when a small British trading post was set up here to barter with the powerful Zulu nation. Originally called Port Natal, the settlement was renamed in 1835 in honour of the Governor of Cape Colony, General Sir Benjamin D'Urban. Despite many vicissitudes, the province of KwaZulu-Natal is the only one where the English language is more widely spoken than Afrikaans.

The personality of Durban is enlivened by its unique population mix: more than 143,000 Indian, 91,200 white and at least 304,000 black (mostly Zulu) and coloured people. As everywhere else in South Africa, the races live to a great

Durban is known in local Zulu as eThekwini – place of the sea

Durban Aquarium

extent in separate areas, they are close enough together to promote something of a cosmopolitan air. Even the black townships are relatively handy to the centre of town. To acknowledge African history, around 200 Durban streets have been renamed, many of them after freedom fighters.

For the tourist, the centre of Durban is the beach. Along the city's **Golden Mile** run – from south to north – uShaka, Addington, South, North and Battery beaches. Closest to the business district, South Beach is usually the most crowded. **North Beach** is the hangout of surfers, with long, rolling waves and a comfortable sea temperature.

For those interested in marine wildlife, a certain highlight of Durban's seafront will be **uShaka Marine World** (www. ushakamarineworld.co.za; daily 9am–5pm). The Sea World zone features an aquarium built into a 1920s cargo steamer, with a large collection of live sharks. There are daily shows featuring dolphins, seals and penguins, and, if you're brave enough, a shark dive tank.

Lined up on **O.R. Tambo Parade** (Marine Parade) are the last surviving rickshaws in Durban. Transplanted here from Japan in Victorian times, the rickshaw quickly became a popular conveyance. Only a handful are left, pulled by Zulus in colourful tribal regalia.

Harbour tours and deep-sea cruises depart from Margaret Mncadi Avenue (the Victoria Embankment), which faces south across Durban Bay. The busy deepwater port–which handles three times the tonnage of Cape Town, South Africa's second biggest port– makes for an interesting outing.

The business district is just a few steps inland from the Victoria Embankment. The **City Hall** Ⓑ is said to be a copy of Belfast's – plus palm trees on either side of the portico. It houses the Public Library, **Durban Art Gallery** and the **Natural Science Museum** (www.durban.gov.za; both Mon–Sat 8.30am–4pm, Sun 11am–4pm; free). In nearby Anton Lembede Street (Smith Street) the **Playhouse** complex (http://playhousecompany.com) houses venues for the performing arts. At the **General Post Office** a plaque commemorates the arrival in Durban in 1899 of the young Winston Churchill after his escape from a Boer prisoner-of-war camp in Pretoria.

The heart of Durban's Indian business district, **Dr Yusuf Dadoo Road** is a lively, exotic area to explore. Although only about 20 percent of the local Indian population is Muslim, the Juma Mosque on Denis Hurley Street is reputed to be the biggest mosque in the southern hemisphere. Its arcades are occupied by shops selling a range of

Gandhi in Durban

Mohandas K. Gandhi, campaigner for Indian independence, first came to Durban in 1893 as a young lawyer and lived here on and off for 21 years, suffering many indignities because of his race. Gandhi conceived his philosophy of non-violent defiance in South Africa, where he led mass protests against discriminatory laws.

delicacies and jewellery, saris (spelt *sarries* in Durban) and European fashions.

Nearby in Joseph Nduli Street (Russell Street), the vast Indian Market (officially the **Victoria Street Market ⊙**) offers a sample of the East. Engaging salesmen all but persuade you to buy enough 'hellfire curry powder' for life. Also on sale are Hindu religious pictures and coral and wood carvings, many of them imported. Watch out for pickpockets.

For a further feel of the tropics, try the Durban **Botanic Gardens** (www.durbanbotanicgardens.org.za; daily 15 Sep–14 Apr 7.30am–5.15pm, winter until 5.30pm; Tea Garden Mon 10am–4pm,Tue–Sun from 9am; free) in St Thomas Road. In the orchid house (9am–5pm) there's a display of orchids, tropical ferns and vines. Outside, acres of lawns are shaded by an incredible variety of trees and elsewhere on the grounds there's a scent garden for the blind.

Golden beaches stretch in endless vistas north and south of Durban. To reach the south coast resorts you have to travel through the port and industrial areas. Sweeping sugar lands eventually materialise (some plantations and factories offer tours), followed by lush vegetation and uncrowded beaches.

The picturesque resort of **Umhlanga Rocks** (18km/11 miles from Durban), with a lighthouse on the beach, is one place where the bathing should be safe – it's the home of the Natal Sharks Board (see page 58).

ZULULAND

North of Durban, the part of KwaZulu-Natal known informally as **Zululand** offers some of the country's best game viewing in an excellent network of provincial and private reserves well suited to self-drive visitors. Other attractions include some fine remote beaches and a number of sites relating to the Zulu monarchy, which originated in the region.

A useful base for exploring this region, **St Lucia Village** overlooks the eponymous 325 sq km (125 sq mile) wetland, which is a Unesco World Heritage Site as the largest estuarine system in Africa. Protected within the **iSimangaliso Wetland Park**  (http://isimangaliso.com), the estuary harbours 800 hippos (the largest population in the country) and a similarly impressive crocodile population, while a checklist of 526 bird species includes pelicans, flamingos, spoonbills, fish eagles and Caspian terns.

A short drive inland of St Lucia, the **Hluhluwe-Imfolozi Game Reserve** ⑩ was proclaimed as two separate entities in 1897, the joint second-oldest game reserves in Africa. Hluhluwe (pronounced shloo-shloo-ee) and Imfolozi (formerly Umfolozi) are now linked by a corridor of state-owned land to create a total area of roughly 1,000 sq km (390 sq miles) in which 81 mammal species have been recorded, including elephant, lion, leopard, cheetah, hunting dog, giraffe, warthog, impala and the localised nyala antelope.

The wetland of St Lucia

Hluhluwe-Imfolozi is best known for its dense rhino populations. In the early 1930s, only about 15 white rhinos were left in southern Africa, but a breeding programme at this reserve succeeded in increasing the local population to 1,600, and

Traditional dress, Shakaland

exporting a further 4,000 of these magnificent animals to other parks. Today, a similar battle is underway to save its cousin, the black rhino, also relatively common here, with an estimated population of 370. Imfolozi's celebrated Wilderness Trail, established in 1957, allows you to explore the region on foot in the company of an armed ranger.

Elephant, rhino, leopard, giraffe and nyala are among the game that you may be able to spot in KZN Wildlife's 36,000-hectare (88,956-acre) **uMkhuze** (formerly Mkuzi) **Game Reserve** (www.kznwildlife. com/mkhuze-park.html), which borders the St Lucia Wetland Park to the east. Mkhuze is celebrated for its tropical birdlife, while photographers are attracted to the hides overlooking its waterholes. Another popular destination with bird-watchers is **Ndumo Game Reserve**, (www.kznwildlife.com/ndumo-park.html) set further north on the border with Mozambique.

Part rundown farmland, part hunting concession before it was acquired by &Beyond (www.andbeyond.com), the private **Phinda Resource Reserve** was subjected to an ambitious programme of reintroductions – lion, cheetah, elephant et al – to boost resident populations of leopard, nyala and other antelope. Phinda today provides an upmarket (and expensive) safari experience to compare with any in Africa. Less luxurious but cheaper is nearby **Zulu Nyala Lodge** (www.zulunyalagroup.com).

At **Shakaland** ⑪ (tel: 035-460 0912; http://aha.co.za/shakaland), a large lodge set about 14km (9 miles) north of

Eshowe, one can enjoy a fascinating Zulu cultural programme for a day, or overnight in a local beehive-style hut with modern lights and plumbing. Two smaller lodges offer a broadly similar experience: **KwaBhekithunga** (tel: 079 903 8903) is a personalised family-run lodge founded some 25 years ago as a craft centre for the disabled, while **Simunye** (tel: 035-450 0101) is an intimate riverside lodge that caters to overnight visitors only.

An important historical site near Ulundi is **Umgungundlovu**, former capital of King Dingane and burial place of the Voortrekker Piet Retief. Also close to Ulundi, the **KwaZulu Cultural Museum and Ondini Historic Reserve** (www.zulu-museum.co.za; Mon–Fri 8am–4pm, Sat–Sun from 9am) is an on-site reconstruction of the capital founded by King Cetshwayo in 1873 and razed six years later by British troops in the last battle of the Anglo-Zulu War. The museum offers

THE ZULUS

Numbering approximately 10 million, Zulus are the largest ethnic African group in South Africa. Once a mighty military power, they famously came into conflict with the Voortrekkers and the British Army in the 19th century. Having often been crudely stereotyped as cattle-herding peasants or bloodthirsty, spear-wielding tribalists, today most view themselves first and foremost as citizens of South Africa. While some live in rural areas of KwaZulu-Natal, where Zulu chiefs play a major role and the cult of the warrior is still prevalent, others are opting for an urban lifestyle, living in suburban areas with middle class jobs, while other, poorer city dwellers live in the townships.

Not all urban Zulus have turned away from their tribal heritage, and many remain faithful to traditional customs, such as a belief in ancestral spirits.

a low-budget version of the Shakaland experience, complete with affordable accommodation in beehive huts.

Farther inland you can visit two other **battlefields** of the 1879 Zulu War: Isandhlwana, where a British force was wiped out; and **Rorke's Drift**, the famous site where a British garrison held out against the Zulus. History buffs can spend weeks tracing the sites, where the Voortrekkers parlayed or fought with the Zulus, and following the progress of the Anglo–Boer War.

From Durban, if you are touring by car, you can head south by way of the coastal resorts and then through Transkei to

SHARKS

A single headline – 'Shark Attacks Swimmer!' – can turn a busy resort into a deserted village, so it's vital to protect the beaches from the deadly species that live in the Indian Ocean. The Natal Sharks Board catches over 1,000 sharks a year. Some 300 huge nets, spread at intervals along 320km (199 miles) of coastline in KwaZulu-Natal, protect 38 beaches.

Even so, the average beach in the province is closed to swimmers 20 days a year. The most dangerous season is from June to August, when sardines migrate close to the shore, attracting so many sharks that the nets are removed to avoid becoming clogged and damaged. The 'sardine run' is now marketed as an attraction in its own right. Those who call the Sardine Hotline (tel: 082-284 9495; June–July) can find out the exact location of sardine activity on the coast and attend the spectacle of shimmering shoals feasted upon by sharks, dolphins and gannets.

An audio-visual show and dissection is presented at the board's offices in the Durban resort of Umhlanga (Tue–Thurs 9am and 2pm, first Sun of the month 2pm; www.shark.co.za).

Tsitsikama, Africa's first coastal national park

East London. From there a transit of the Ciskei region brings you to Grahamstown and Port Elizabeth. Some tour companies offer trips inland to visit game and nature reserves, where you can hunt, hike or watch the wildlife. Alternatively, you can tour on your own. Malarial precautions are needed for some areas; contact the KwaZulu-Natal Tourism Authority (see page 127).

THE SOUTHERN COAST

South Africa's southern coast is a picturesque patchwork of beaches, forests and lakes. Inland attractions include the Addo Elephant Park, ostrich ranches and the Cango Caves.

PORT ELIZABETH

The country's motor industry is concentrated in **Port Elizabeth** (often called PE) and, perhaps fittingly, the centre of the city is crossed by a network of elevated super-highways, isolating the business district from the harbour. But there is more to Port Elizabeth than first impressions suggest. About 2km (1.5 miles) south of the centre is **King's Beach**, popular with surfers and swimmers. Beyond, along Humewood Beach, the **Bayworld complex** (www.bayworld.co.za; daily 9am–4.30pm) features a fine anthropological and natural history museum and an oceanarium.

Next door is Bayworld's snake park, where a seemingly care-free handler wraps himself in puff adders and mambas while reciting a speech on the art of avoiding snakebites. Also nearby is The Boardwalk (www.suninternational.com), a beachfront complex with casino, restaurants, shops and cinema.

With a little imagination, you can picture Port Elizabeth as it must have been 60 years ago when the Campanile was built. The bell tower, 52m (171ft) tall and reminiscent of the one in Venice, has a 23-bell carillon (closed for renovation at the time of writing).

The **business district**, with big modern department stores, is what you'd expect in a city of more than half a million people. Main Street starts at the Mayor's Garden and the City Hall, a national monument dating from 1858. After a fire in 1977 the interior was re-done in a sparkling modern style, though no less stately than the building's exterior. A statue of Queen Victoria, facing the harbour, marks the main public library, which is beautiful and worth a look. A tourist office is also found here.

Inside the park

Roads inside Addo Elephant National Park pass near several waterholes where elephants are likely to appear in dry weather. Getting out of your car anywhere inside the enclosure is forbidden, except at designated lookout points, where visitors may exit their vehicle at their own risk. Another road along the outside has elevated viewing points. For more information visit www.sanparks.org/parks/addo.

ADDO ELEPHANT PARK

An hour's drive from Port Elizabeth, the descendants of the last elephants to live wild in Cape Province thrive in the **Addo Elephant National Park** , which must surely rank as one of the best destinations in Africa for elephant watching. More than 600 remarkably relaxed pachyderms roam the park now.

During your visit, you might also glimpse lions, black rhino, buffalo and several types of antelope. Restricting visibility, though, is the evergreen addo bush,

Addo elephant and calf

which is short but impenetrable. Among all the tangled creepers are beautiful midget trees–wonderfully bright when in flower.

The Addo elephants won world attention in the 1920s. Stalking valuable farm land, they terrified local residents and damaged crops. A famous hunter, Major Pretorius, was contracted to exterminate the herd. In a period of almost a year, he killed 120, but 15 of the most cunning elephants eluded him. Public sympathy subsequently welled up for the victims and the survivors were thus reprieved. Setting up a national park for them was easier than confining them. Various types of fencing were tried and failed, until a high fence of tram rails and steel cables was devised. The park now covers an area of 180,000 hectares (444,700 acres).

THE GARDEN ROUTE

Beacon Isle Hotel, Central Beach, Plettenberg

The N2 highway links Port Elizabeth and Cape Town. Composed of many kinds of landscape, exactly which stretch of this road deserves the semi-official title of the **Garden Route** is somewhat vague. The most attractive section of the route runs about 220km (137 miles) between the mouth of the Storms River and Mossel Bay.

West from Port Elizabeth, **Jeffrey's Bay** is considered to be South Africa's surfing paradise, well known to the international surfing set, who arrive in March for the new season. All year round the pink arc of sand is a delight. The beach is also a treasure trove of seashells, as you'll see in the **shell museum** (Mon–Sat 9am–4pm, Sun 9am–1pm) in the library on the seafront.

In majestic countryside to the west, a splendid national park is centred near the Storms River. An ingenious and graceful bridge with a span of 192m (630ft) offers a formidable view down the gorge to the river far below. On the landward side of the N2 is the **Tsitsikama National Park** (www.sanparks.org), with trees such as yellowwood, stinkwood and candlewood. Hiking trails are laid out to provide surveys of the big trees, the ferns and lichen, and the wild flowers.

Across the highway the park continues for about 80km (50 miles) along the rugged shore. The first coastal national park on the continent of Africa, it's a sanctuary for otters, bushbacks and vervet monkeys, along with 280 species of birds.

The restricted zone extends half a mile into the ocean, protecting dolphins, whales and the marine environment. The 42-km (25-mile) Otter Trail, leads hikers along the coastline over cliffs, through forests and across streams.

The Garden Route offers some sensational scenery: pine and eucalyptus trees stretch endlessly behind blossoming roadside trees; tortuous stretches of road pass through and over gorges; the ocean appears in sudden glimpses between sheer cliffs.

When the Portuguese navigators of the 15th century saw **Plettenberg Bay** ⑬ they were moved to call it Bahia Formosa (Beautiful Bay)–a judgement today's traveller would find hard to disagree with. The vast, classic arc of sandy beach is a favourite with visitors from far and near. The cape that protects the bay, called Robberg (Seal Mountain), supports a nature reserve that's accessible on foot.

A ringtail lemur and tourist

Wooden masks for sale

The premier attraction in the region is **Monkeyland** (www.monkeyland.co.za; daily 8am–5pm), a refuge for abused and abandoned primates. East of Plett along the N2 is the **Elephant Sanctuary** (www.elephant sanctuary.co.za), where you can ride pachyderms and learn all about them.

On the way from Plettenberg Bay to Knysna is the **Garden of Eden**, a primeval forest. The sun's rays are barely able to filter through interwoven branches of trees that were here long before the coast was first sighted.

The Knysna forests (www.sanparks.org) cover 80,000 hectares (197,600 acres), and are as valuable as they are beautiful. They were badly diminished in the 19th and early 20th centuries by reckless exploitation. With timberland constituting barely one percent of South Africa's total area, this resource is now carefully controlled by the government.

The town of **Knysna** (the 'K' is silent) is a popular resort that possesses an intriguing history. It was founded by George Rex, widely believed to be an illegitimate son of King George III of England. After arriving from the Cape at the beginning of the 19th century, he bought a big farm along the Knysna lagoon and turned the district into a seaport and a shipbuilding and timber centre. Boats and furniture are still made in Knysna, although the port lost its commercial importance. **The Heads**, a famous rocky beauty spot, marks the dramatic entry of the Indian Ocean into Knysna's lagoon. The lagoon stretches far inland and provides ideal conditions for anglers and sailors alike. An unusual landmark along the lagoon is **Holy Trinity Church** at Belvidere (www.holytrinitybelvidere. org), built in the 19th century along the lines of a Norman church. It's one of the smallest churches in South Africa, with room for only 65 people.

More lagoons, lakes, timberland and voluptuously moulded hills characterise the Garden Route west of Knysna. The next resort along the highway, **Wilderness**, is not as deserted as its name suggests, offering hotels, camping sites and caravan parks, although there are also miles of unspoiled beaches.

George, the regional centre and airport hub at the intersection of the Garden Route and a main road to the Little Karoo, was named after George Rex's putative father, King George. The finest structure in this plateau municipality of 193,000 is an impressive **Dutch Reformed Church** (www.caw.org.za) blindingly white and of dignified proportions. The **Outeniqua Choo-Tjoe** steam train used to run from George to Mossel Bay. The local Transport **Museum** (www.outeniqua chootjoe.co.za; Sept–Apr Mon–Sat 8am–7pm, May–Aug Mon–Fri 8am–4.30pm, Sat until 2pm) boasts a collection of steam engines, including the Emil Kessler-Johannesburg's first steam locomotive.

Ostrich farm tour

THE LITTLE KAROO

In strangely beautiful semi-desert beyond the Outeniqua Mountains, about 56km (35 miles) inland from George, **Oudtshoorn** ⓮ is the capital of the Little Karoo. A stroll along any shopping street will soon show you what's different about this place. The stores sell ostrich feathers of many colours, empty ostrich eggs, dried ostrich meat, ostrich-hide wallets–even lamps and ashtrays standing on ostrich feet. Ostriches are big business here.

The **ostrich ranches** on the outskirts of town offer an inimitable experience. In their thousands, nature's mightiest birds strut and scratch or stand about with vacant expressions in their bulging eyes. Guided tours of the farms cover the history of the Little Karoo's 90,000-strong herd, the boom of the Victorian era when ostrich feathers sold for 500 rand per kg (2.2lbs) and even tell you how to hatch an ostrich egg. There are ostrich races, in which the fleet, muscular, earth-bound bird have to run with 'jockeys' on their backs.

Why Oudtshoorn? It seems ostriches are happiest in a hot, dry climate; they like the type of alfalfa grown here and the availability of their favourite diet supplements–sand, stones and insects.

About 26km (16 miles) north of Oudtshoorn, in the foothills of the Swartberg (Black Mountain), is another popular attraction, the **Cango Caves** (www.cango-caves. co.za; daily, hourly guided tours; advance booking required). They're easy to reach over a mountain road

Whale watching

The Western Cape whale route is active from June to September, affording visitors incredible views of migrating whales. Sometimes the giant sea mammals have passed so close to shore that onlookers have been soaked by their mighty spray. A popular spot for whale watching is at Hermanus, where a 'whale crier' blows a horn to alert spectators.

Cango Caves, Oudtshoorn

that mostly follows a meandering river, its banks fringed by weeping willows. The caves once sheltered Bushmen, whose paintings were found on the walls. The last resort on the seaside section of the Garden Route is **Mossel Bay**, a working seaport with some beaches and natural swimming pools among the rocks. Sailing ships visited the bay as early as 1488, when the Portuguese navigator Bartolomeu Dias became the first European to touch South African soil. The **Bartolomeu Dias Museum Complex** (http://diasmuseum.co.za; Mon–Fri 9am–4.45pm, Sat and Sun 9am–3.45pm), housed inside a converted granary, is dedicated to his memory. Displays include a full-scale replica of Dias' surprisingly small caravel. The first permanent settlement at Mossel Bay was established some 300 years later, although passing ships often stopped for water and to trade with the local Hottentots.

The road to Cape Town heads away from the coast to **Swellendam**, one of the Cape's first inland towns. It has a curious past – declared independence from the Dutch East

Indies Company in 1795, only to submit to the British the year after. Some fine buildings date from the 18th century and the wool boom of the 19th century. Close by, **Bontebok National Park** (www.sanparks.org) is home to the rare bontebok and other antelopes.

CAPE TOWN

One of the great experiences for any traveller is the first sight of **Cape Town's** ⓑ classic combination of cloud-topped mountain, skyscrapered flatland and the Atlantic Ocean.

Although the climate suits pines, palms and frangipani, and the winters are mild, it rains a lot and, in summer, a southeasterly wind assails the city. Called the Cape Doctor, it is credited with sweeping away germs, mosquitoes and air pollution. During this season, Table Mountain acquires its 'tablecloth'–a strip of cloud that hovers over the summit.

Cape Town is surrounded by a breathtaking barrier of mountains

Cape Town's main street, **Adderley Street Ⓐ**, runs along the modern façade of the railway terminus. Between the station and the docks, the zone called the Foreshore has been reclaimed from the sea and is now occupied by an overpowering array of elevated highways and buildings. The pedestrian mall on St George's Street hosts traditional marimba dance displays at lunchtime and on Saturday morning.

The giant **Civic Centre** straddling Hertzog Boulevard houses the **Artscape Theatre Centre**, (www.artscape.co.za), with up-to-date technology behind the scenes.

CITY CENTRE

Pedestrians make their way underground on the landward side of the railway station. In the passage beneath Strand Street is the tourist information office (www.capetown.travel). There's also an old postal stone, under which 17th-century sailors put letters to be picked up by homeward-bound ships.

Trafalgar Place, off Adderley Street, is the site of Cape Town's outdoor flower market, run by women of the Malay community. The Cape Malays are mostly the descendants of slaves brought from Southeast Asia in the late 17th century. They are Muslims and some still live in the **Malay Quarter**, or **Bo-Kaap**, near the business district (beyond Buitengracht Street). It's worth seeing the pastel-coloured houses, steep cobbled streets and minarets, as well as the Jamai (or Queen Victoria) Mosque, Cape Town's oldest, dating back to 1850. Ironically, the character of the Malay Quarter is now threatened by the end of residence restrictions, as well-heeled outsiders try to buy up property here. To learn more, visit the **Bo-Kaap Museum** (www.iziko.org.za).

Most of Cape Town's inhabitants are Cape Coloured: of mixed descent involving early white settlers, Hottentots and indigenous blacks or imported slaves. They outnumber the whites by

Township tours

The townships that cover the sandy flats east of Cape Town were created under apartheid, when tens of thousands of 'non-white' Capetonians were forcibly evicted from more central suburbs. As a result, popular 'township tours' led by local residents, are now offered by most Cape Town operators.

nearly two to one. The black population of Cape Town is small, amounting to one in eight residents. Most of Cape Town's black community are Xhosa speakers; listen for the amazing clicking sounds in their conversation.

Cape Town **City Hall**, an Italian Renaissance-type palace from the early 20th century, faces the **Grand Parade**, once used as a parade ground for troops. Before that the Dutch East Indies Company's first building in the Cape stood on this spot–an earthwork fort of 1652. Now the Parade is a large car park, with a fruit and flower market and, every Wednesday and Saturday morning, a flea market. Beware of pickpockets here.

Beyond the Grand Parade stands the **Castle of Good Hope** (www.castleofgoodhope.co.za; guided tours Mon–Sat at 11am, noon, 2pm), the oldest building in South Africa, a sturdy, pentagonal fortress surrounded by a restored moat and inviting gardens. Guides explain the tactical layout and show off the dungeons. The castle contains small military and maritime museums and the William Fehr Collection of paintings, Cape silver and furniture and Asian porcelain. The Key Ceremony (the unlocking of the Castle) is performed from Mon – Fri at 10am and noon.

Facing on to the cobbled **Greenmarket Square** **B**, the **Old Town House** is a grand Baroque building dating from 1761 that served as the city hall until 1905. Now it holds the Michaelis Collection of Dutch and Flemish art (www.iziko.org.za), including a treasured Frans Hals portrait and dozens of oils by his contemporaries. The **Groote Kerk** (Great Church;

http://grootekerk.org.za), at the point where Adderley Street runs into pedestrianised Government Avenue, is sometimes called the oldest church in South Africa. The clock tower dates from 1703 and the rest was rebuilt much later.

Government Avenue, an oak-shaded gravel walk nearly a kilometre long, runs down the middle of the original Dutch East Indies Company's **Garden**, laid out by the first governor, Jan Van Riebeeck. Here, some 300 slaves produced fruit and vegetables for settlers and the visiting ships of the Company. About one-third of the original farm area has been turned into a resplend-ent botanical garden; the rest is occupied by buildings like the South African Houses of Parliament (www.parliament.gov.za; tours Mon–Fri 9am–noon).

Several cultural institu-tions are sited around here, including the **South African National Gallery**  (www.iziko.org.za; daily 10am–5pm), which highlights the work of both South African and English artists.

At the market, Cape Town

Nearby, the **Jewish Mus-eum** (www.sajewishmuseum.org.za; Sun–Thur 10am– 5pm, Fri until 2pm) occupies the Greek-columned building of South Africa's first ever synagogue (1862); next door is the twin-towered Gardens Synagogue.

Dioramas of natural his-tory and prehistoric life, plus Bushmen rock paintings,

are on show at the **South African Museum** (www.iziko.org.
za; daily 10am–5pm), the oldest institution of its kind in the
country. Nearby, located in an elegant Edwardian house, is
the New Church Museum (http://thenewchurch.co), the first
private contemporary art museum in Cape Town.

DOCKS AND HARBOUR

The port area starts close to the city centre, but it's so big you
may want to explore it by car. Probably the best way to see the
fleets of banana boats, fishing trawlers and container ships is
on a harbour cruise or a trip round Table Bay.

The ambitious development scheme for the two oldest dock
basins at the **Victoria & Alfred Waterfront** ⓓ (www.water
front.co.za) has revitalised the area, creating a complex of
restaurants, shops and entertainment centres, the South
African Maritime Museum, an interactive rugby museum and

Waterfront, Cape Town

a hotel set in a former warehouse. The area has now become the Cape's biggest magnet for visitors, although it remains a busy working port. One of the country's premier cultural institutions, the Zeitz Museum of Contemporary Art Africa(Zeitz MOCAA; www.zeitzfoundation.org), is due to open in 2017.

A highlight of a visit to the waterfront is the **Two Oceans Aquarium** (daily 9.30am–6pm; www.aquarium.co.za), which brims with marine life of all shapes and dimensions, from seahorses and sea urchins to great white sharks and Cape fur seals.

TABLE MOUNTAIN

People have been climbing **Table Mountain** Ⓔ at least since 1503, when the Portuguese mariner Antonio de Saldanha went up to check the lie of the land and sea. Today, climbers can choose from 350 routes to the 1,087-m (3,565-ft) summit of the shale, sandstone and granite flattop. The climb can be dangerous, however, so amateurs are warned to start early, be certain of the weather and dress suitably. Guides are available to show you the way.

Alternatively, you can take the easy way –in seven minutes. The cable car has been whisking passengers to the top, and down again, since 1929. There's plenty of room on top to roam, with maps and telescopes there. If the weather starts to deteriorate, a siren recalls visitors to the cable car station for a return to earth before service is suspended. In good weather, the cars operate half hourly from May–Aug 8.30am until 4.30pm, Sep–Oct 6pm, Nov and Feb 7pm, 1–15 Dec and 16–31 Jan 7.30pm, 16 Dec–15 Jan 8.30pm, Mar 6.30pm, Apr 5.30pm (www.tablemountain.net). If you're using public transport, take the red City Sightseeing bus from outside the Two Oceans Aquarium. See www.citysightseeing.co.za for a timetable and other bus stop locations.

THE CAPE PENINSULA

The Cape of Good Hope is as gripping a part of the world as you'll ever see and the sights on the way are worth stopping for. There are two likely routes for exploring around the 50-km (31-mile) long peninsula. The more leisurely one starts out along the coast, counterclockwise from central Cape Town and the waterfront, passing South Africa's oldest working lighthouse at **Green Point**. Ferries make the 11.5-km (7-mile) trip out to **Robben Island**, which has been converted into a living museum and is a Unesco World Heritage Site. It's interesting for its flora and African (or jackass) penguins, but famous for Nelson Mandela's imprisonment here. Groups are limited, so bookings must be made in advance (www.robben-island.org.za).

Sea Point is an in-town beach resort with a fashionable promenade and high-rent, high-rise buildings of all kinds of architectural style. For miles beyond, the road reveals beach after beach alternating with rocky coves. Clifton Bay, with four beaches, is the most popular. The season is at its height from mid-October to mid-March. Along the Atlantic Coast, however, the water is cold all year round. For tolerable sea temperatures, visit the opposite shore of the peninsula and the warmer waters of False Bay.

A cell, Robben Island

The road soon turns inland along the slopes of the **Twelve Apostles** mountain formation. The highway returns to sea level at the big semi-circular fishing harbour of **Hout Bay**. Although some yachts are moored here, Hout Bay is obviously a working port. At certain times of the year the industrial aspects

Chapman's Peak Drive

overwhelm the scenery, when factories producing fish meal and fish oil emit their vapours. Hout Bay is also an important source of a South African delicacy, smoked *snoek*, and there are some good seafood restaurants.

A favourite excursion from here is by launch to some rocks known as **Duiker Island** ⑯, out beyond the calm of the harbour. Hundreds of seals can be seen diving and playing. Cormorants, gulls and oystercatchers perch wing to wing on available spaces.

Past Hout Bay, the Marine Drive rises to its climax–a corniche that hangs between cliffs and sea. When **Chapman's Peak Drive** (www.chapmanspeakdrive.co.za) was undertaken during World War I, it was considered to be a breakthrough in road engineering. There is a lookout point at the highest spot on the drive. The route soon swerves inland and crosses the Cape Peninsula, now hardly 10km (6 miles) wide. At the eastern extremity lies the small town of **Fish Hoek**, a good spot for swimming.

The other way from Cape Town to Fish Hoek is by the inland route. The M3 highway exits town as a busy but well-landscaped boulevard, passing the Groote Schuur Hospital, where, in 1967, Professor Christiaan Barnard led the team that performed the first transplant of a human heart.

On the slopes of Devil's Peak, the **Rhodes Memorial** is an impressive monument to the controversial financier/states-man, lambasted by some contemporary historians as a white supremacist and an architect of apartheid. In a simulated Greek Temple at the top of cascading granite steps, a bust of Cecil Rhodes looks out over what was his favourite view.

The oldest university in South Africa is set in priceless for-ested surroundings beneath Devil's Peak. The University of Cape Town (www.uct.ac.za), founded in 1829, has both tradi-tional, ivy-covered buildings and stark modern ones, includ-ing the Baxter Theatre (www.baxter.co.za), an intellectual focus for the city as well as for the university.

About 3km (2 miles) past the UCT campus it's a short side trip off the M3 to **Kirstenbosch** (www.sanbi.org/gardens/kirstenbosch; daily Apr–Aug 8am–6pm; Sept–Mar 8am–7pm), a renowned botanical garden. Thousands of plant species grow here – representing nearly a quarter of the types found in South Africa. From August to early October is the most exciting time to visit.

CAPE DUTCH

Dramatic landscapes add to the visual impact of the Cape's old country seats – large white houses, often with thatched roofs. Cape Dutch architecture features symmetrical gables with curves and baroque intricacies, window shutters, wide main doors with fanlights and airy interiors with timbered ceilings.

One of the most magnificent Cape Dutch houses – **Groot Constantia**, (www.grootconstantia.co.za) south of Kirstenbosch – is now a living museum. Since the turn of the 18th century, this farm has been producing great wines. Part of the old cellars, behind the main house, has been turned into a wine museum. The main museum, which occupies the homestead itself, includes antique furniture, porcelain, implements and glassware.

An elegant Cape Dutch mansion

FALSE BAY

To make the most of a tour round the peninsula's coast, set out early, as the sun rises above the Hottentots-Holland Mountains and shimmers on the surface of **False Bay**. About 30km (19 miles) wide, the bay has a number of tantalising beaches.

Situated 20km (12 miles) from the centre of Cape Town, on the east coast, is the booming resort of **Muizenberg** ⑰, with endless dunes of almost snow-white sand. The sea here is good for swimming between November and April.

The suburban railway from Cape Town will take you to **Simon's Town**, the main base of the South African navy. You can spot frigates and mine sweepers here and many a desirable yacht. An unusual monument to Simonstown's past as a British naval base is the **Martello Tower**, somewhat hidden from view inside the dockyard area. This cylindrical stone fort, built in 1796, is thought to be the oldest of its kind in the world.

Even though lighthouses, paved roads and a restaurant have been added, the **Cape of Good Hope** sector of the recently proclaimed **Table Mountain National Park** (www.sanparks.org), remains virtually intact in its primeval state. Driving along the lesser roads you might come across the rare bontebok, as well as eland, springbok, ostrich and other wildlife. Baboons, unfortunately, are legion. Signs warn visitors not to feed them (and if you leave your car, lock it up with the windows closed as baboons loot from unsecured vehicles). Specialists are fascinated by the flora – mostly low shrubs and grass. Everyone enjoys the outbursts of colour from wild protea and heather.

The reserve's long coastline varies from cliffs to rocky flats and sandy coves, but the high spot is where the roads run out, at **Cape Point ⓰** (http://capepoint.co.za). A small tram called the Flying Dutchman shuttles visitors from the car park (parking lot) to the top of the final hill. From there you can walk to various observation points, the highest at the base of the original 1860 lighthouse. The new 19 million-candle lighthouse is purportedly the most powerful in the world.

At Cape Point, the granite cliffs plunge 259m (850ft) to the sea – South Africa's tallest sea cliffs. Giant rollers boil and froth at the base, while cormorants fight the shrieking wind to reach their ledges. Albatross, gannets, gulls and giant petrels share the fishing in this tormented sea.

Looking west, you see the Cape of Good Hope itself, not Africa's southernmost tip, which is actually Cape Agulhas near Bredasdorp, but still spectacular. The spot is accessible from the road, so you can climb the rocks near sea level for a closer look at the breaking waves.

Cape of storms

Searching for the route to India, the Portuguese explorer Bartolomeu Dias rounded the Cape for the first time in 1488. Unable to see it due to a raging storm, he wrote on his map, 'Cape of Storms'. Although it was later renamed the Cape of Good Hope, Dias was lost at sea in the same waters 12 years later.

Good Hope Nature Reserve

WINE COUNTRY

South African wines originate in a small corner of the country within a 162-km (100-mile) radius of Cape Town. The soils and microclimates within this arc are so varied that all manner of wines can be produced, from sweet and dry whites to rosés, reds and fortified types in the style of sherry and port.

One-day excursions offered by tour operators cover two principal centres, Stellenbosch and Paarl. The tourist information offices of both regions issue maps and brochures and can suggest itineraries. The scenery itself is enchanting.

STELLENBOSCH

Less than 50km (31 miles) east of central Cape Town, **Stellenbosch** ⓳ has a wealth of beautiful old buildings. It's an endearing, relaxed university town named after the great 17th-century wine enthusiast, Governor Van der Stel. Fires destroyed the original thatched cottages and the best of the buildings on view today date from between 1775 and 1820.

Wine cellar

A visit to the **Stellenbosch Village Museum**, (http://stelmus.co.za) consisting of four houses, each from different period in the history of the town, is a must. **Grosvenor House**, an early 19th-century mansion with an award-winning garden, is filled with Old Cape furnishings. **Schreuder House** (1709), with simple settlers' furnishings, is possibly the country's oldest surviving town house. At the end of Dorn Street a homestead of 1780 houses the **Rembrandt Van Rijn Art Gallery**. In the same compound a wine museum displays old Roman amphoras and antique glasses and bottles. Nearby is a museum featuring the history and technology of brandy-making.

Around Stellenbosch, vineyards spread for miles over hillsides and valleys, against a backdrop of imposing mountains. About 50 **wine estates** and cooperatives in the district welcome visitors daily (some close on Saturday afternoon and Sunday), usually offering scheduled cellar tours, wine tastings and opportunities to buy. Look out for the 'Wine Route' logo.

On Stellenbosch's outskirts, **Rustenberg Wine Estate** (www.rustenberg.co.za), with its orchards and gabled dairy, is one of the most beautiful in the Cape. As is **Vergelegen** (www.vergelegen.co.za), whose name means 'Far Away', referring to its location on the once remote footslopes of the Helderberg Mountains south of Stellenbosch. Founded in

1700, the manor house, decorated in period style, is a fine example of Cape Dutch architecture.

To the southwest, **Franschhoek** (literally French Corner) is named after the Huguenots, who settled there in the 18th century. Framed by lofty blue peaks, Franschhoek is ideal for an al fresco lunch, either in town, or at historic **Boschendal Estate** (www.boschendal.com), where you can picnic before visiting the cellars.

PAARL

The Cape's other main wine region centres on the 18th-century town of **Paarl**, about 60km (37 miles) from Cape Town, just off the N1 motorway. It's about twice the size of Stellenbosch, with a huge modern civic centre that also houses the information office. The long main street is lined with historic buildings, working vineyards and the headquarters of KWV, the Cooperative Wine Growers Association. Tours are scheduled four times a day. The **Old Parsonage (Oude Pastorie) Museum**,

CAPE WINE

Stellenbosch and Paarl, the main and probably most versatile of the Cape wine regions, offer the best of everything: rich reds, crisp whites, ports in true Portuguese style, Sauterne-like sweet Noble Late Harvest wines and some excellent value-for-money Cap Classiques.

Franschhoek, a valley of boutique wineries, offers mostly white wines, with a handful of red gems. Then there's Constantia, with a select range of classical whites and reds nurtured in historic Cape Dutch cellars. Walker Bay is the place for some of the Cape's benchmark Pinot Noirs and Chardonnays, and a taste of pioneering Pinotages.

in a perfectly restored, 18th-century Cape Dutch building, has a fine collection of old Cape furniture and silver.

Elsewhere in Paarl and the surrounding Berg River Valley are numerous **wine estates** and cooperative cellars. Most have wines for sale, with or without tastings, and cellar tours either on a schedule or by arrangement.

The more time you have, the more treasures you will be able to discover in this part of the Cape. **Ceres**, a pretty town at the heart of a rich fruit-growing region, is well worth a visit; and **Tulbagh ⓳**, which dates from the early 18th century, has some of the most beautiful Cape Dutch houses of all.

CAPE TOWN TO JOHANNESBURG

You can fly back to Johannesburg, of course, but if you have time you'll see more of the country by driving or taking the

THE BLUE TRAIN

The 1,608-km (997-mile), 26-hour journey on the Blue Train between Cape Town and Pretoria via Johannesburg is one of the world's most luxurious. A five-star hotel on wheels, it offers three-room suites–lounge, bedroom and bathroom–or simpler quarters. The designers thought of everything: a thin layer of gold on the double windows reduces heat and glare; venetian blinds between the panes operate electrically; and air springs guarantee a quiet, smooth ride.

After a champagne farewell, the 16-car train sets off. Lounge in the bar, dine handsomely (the price includes meals) and gaze outside as Table Mountain and the Cape vineyards gradually give way to the semi-desert of the Great Karoo. The approach to Johannesburg is indicated by the truncated pyramids of gold-mine waste heaps. For reservations tel: 012-334 8459; www.bluetrain.co.za.

train, either the regular service or the luxury Blue Train.

The railway and the direct
road both cross **Great Karoo**,
a vast semi-desert. Despite
a lack of rainfall, some fascinating forms of plant life
are able to flourish here and
in places water is pumped up
from bore holes to sustain
the flocks of sheep. If you're

Augrabies Falls

travelling by car, **Kimberley**
❷❶ is a convenient overnight stop. The former mining town's
famous **Big Hole** is about 1.5km (1 mile) round and half as
deep, the excavation at the top of this 'pipe' from the earth's
depths was the source of over 14 million carats of diamonds
between 1871 and 1914.

It looks far on the map, but good roads and light traffic
mean that the journey from the Cape to Jo'burg is an easy
two-day trip. An alternative to the shortest route involves
only a few hours' more driving. Head north up the Western
Cape through lovely scenery (and in September, spectacular wild flowers) to **Springbok**, then east via **Upington**. It's
a short diversion to the **Augrabies Falls**, where the Orange
River thunders over the escarpment, forming one of the
world's great waterfalls.

South Africa's strangest extremity is its piece of the
Kalahari Desert. A tongue of territory jutting out between
Namibia and Botswana, the **Kgalagadi Transfrontier
Park** ❷❷ (www.sanparks.org) is reached by dusty but well-
graded roads. The park has excellent accommodation and
other facilities. While here, you may catch sight of gems-
bok, springbok, lions and, if you're lucky, cheetahs, too.

WHAT TO DO

SPORTS

South Africans are dedicated to the outdoor life. Half the country seems to be wielding fishing rods or golf clubs, running, swimming or riding surfboards. The other half is likely to be watching cricket, rugby, football, wrestling or racing. In general, sporting stars tend to receive more publicity and acclaim than film celebrities or politicians. South African Tourism (see page 127) can provide useful details about sporting activities and tour operations.

WATERSPORTS

South Africa's 2,800km (1,740 miles) of coastline caters for all tastes. In parts of KwaZulu-Natal and the Eastern and Western Cape, dunes stretch endlessly into total wilderness. If you prefer convenience and crowds, the popular resorts have all the facilities. Because of sharks and tricky tides, swim only where signs indicate it's safe. The busier beaches have lifeguards on duty in summer. If the waves are too high or the sea is uncomfortably cold (as the Atlantic often is), you can fall back on the hotel swimming pool.

Surfing has become a South African passion. The waves of the Eastern Cape are fit for champions, with often impeccable conditions to be found at Cape St Francis and Jeffrey's Bay, and warmer waters in the Durban area. For information, contact the United Surfing Council of South Africa: www.surfingsouthafrica.co.za.

Windsurfing (boardsailing) is the fastest-growing water sport in South Africa, from the Indian Ocean to the chilly Atlantic (where wetsuits are standard) and on lakes inland.

Fishing, Kalk Bay

Check with the South African Windsurfing Class Association (www.windsurfingafrica.org) for those areas that require permits for offshore windsurfing. Old-fashioned sailing hasn't lost its allure, with dozens of yacht clubs offering facilities and classes at all levels.

For still more varied thrills, **white-water rafting** trips are offered on the stretch of the Orange River near Augrabies Falls; contact the Kalahari Adventure Centre (tel: 082-476 8213, www.kalahari-adventures.co.za) for details. You'll find good **scuba diving** schools and clubs in the vicinity of all the main coastal resorts. Contact the South African Underwater Sport Federation (www.cmas.co.za).

Surfers on the beach, Port Elizabeth

FISHING

Whether they prefer rock, surf, or deep-sea fishing, anglers will have a field day in South Africa. Everything they could dream of can be found in the South Atlantic and Indian oceans. The oceans' meeting point, near Cape Town, is said to be the home of more kinds of game fish than any other sea; for instance, all species of marlin and tunny (tuna) have been landed here. In the big ports, such as Cape Town and Durban, you can join organised **deep-sea excursions**. Elsewhere, small, powerful ski boats may be hired to reach the action.

The best seasons for rock and surf fishing vary with the region. In the Western Cape, it's from January to April, but along the Kwa-Zulu-Natal coast the most promising time is from June to November. There is unparalleled excitement in June between Port St Johns and Durban: immense

Go fishing

Inland, rivers and lakes all over the country offer the chance to fish for trout, bass, and carp. There are strict catch limits in most places and permits are required; contact the local parks board or Department of Nature Conservation for permit and catch requirements.

shoals of sardines run along the coast, attracting shark, barracuda, kingfish and shad, which in turn lure anglers to the scene. If you want to join the crayfish (rock lobster) hunt, you will need a licence, and there are seasonal restrictions for these and for oysters and abalone (here called *perlemoen*).

PARTICIPATION SPORTS

Saturday is the most important day of the week for organised sports in South Africa. While for many years sporting activities of any importance were banned on Sundays, games are played regularly on this day, too.

Golf has been played in South Africa for well over a century and there are several courses of international repute. Many courses welcome visitors, at least on weekdays, when even the public courses are not normally overcrowded. It's worth contacting club secretaries for starting times and to check dress codes. The South African Golf Association can also advise: www.saga.co.za. Golf is played all the year round, but over most of the country the greens are at their best from December to March. Carry an umbrella for those inevitable afternoon rainstorms.

The good weather makes year-round **tennis** a possibility, too. The equivalent of Wimbledon in South Africa,

Ellis Park in Johannesburg has 21 tennis courts. The Wanderers (www.thewanderersclub.co.za) is one of more than 170 tennis clubs in the city and has 26 courts. Most of the resort hotels either have their own courts or else have access to facilities nearby; for more information call the South African Tennis Association (tel: 011-442 0500, www. tennissa.co.za). In addition, some of the hotels also have **squash** courts.

The tranquil-looking, but nevertheless highly competitive, British game of **bowls** arrived early in South Africa, spreading from Port Elizabeth to KwaZulu-Natal and the Rand. Today 60,000 bowlers belong to some 800 clubs; visiting players from abroad are welcomed.

A growing interest in the **martial arts** has an obvious link with self-defence in the city streets. **Mountain biking** has become as much a passion with the young as it has in many

Mountain biking in the Swartberg Mountains

Western countries, but a game called **jukskei** seems to be home-grown: in the same way that Americans throw horse shoes at a peg, Afrikaners have taken to throwing sticks.

OUTDOOR ACTIVITIES

Horse riding and associated sports take place across the republic. The Johannesburg area alone has 20 riding schools, and out in the wilds

Extreme sports

South Africa's varied and often dramatic landscape offers plenty of opportunities for unusual and extreme activities. You could try sandboarding down huge coastal dunes (tel: 021-422 0388, www.downhill adventures.com) or bungee jumping from Bloukrans Bridge, the highest in Africa (tel: 042-281 1458, www.faceadrenalin.com.

some country hotels have their own stables. Pony treks are arranged by KZN Wildlife (tel: 033-845 1999, www.kznwildlife. com) in the uKhahlamba-Drakensberg.

A series of **hiking** trails has been developed (there are over 1000 registered routes across the country) which reach from the mountains of the Cape to the northern Transvaal. For information about hiking in this region, tel: 012 329 0462/072 476 8438 or see www.magalieshiking.co.za.

It's quite costly, but you can go **hot-air ballooning** in the Magaliesberg Mountains near Johannesburg or in the Drakensberg Mountains, KwaZulu-Natal, where you'll also see hang gliders doing their stuff. In fact, if any form of sport or exercise catches on anywhere in the world, you can be sure that it will soon find popularity in South Africa.

The successful conservation of the game herds means that for some species there has to be a culling programme, and this opens up the possibility of **hunting**. Details of quotas and costs and other information can be obtained from South African Tourism (see page 127).

SPECTATOR SPORTS

Horse racing takes place year-round at tracks in all the major cities. The race of the year is the Durban July Handicap, which is run on the first Saturday of July. For more details visit the website of the Racing Association (www.racingassociation.co.za).

The **motor racing** circuit at Kyalami, north of Johannesburg, hosts a range of motor and motorbike racing events throughout the year.

Rugby, **cricket** and **football** have practically attained religious status among participants and spectators alike. Although efforts are being made to provide black South Africans with better playing facilities, rugby is still a predominantly white pursuit. You can see top-class matches at the huge Ellis Park stadium in Johannesburg, at Greenpoint Stadium in Cape Town, and indeed in every city and town throughout the winter. Other

A NATIONAL PASSION

Today sport in South Africa is able to transcend race and politics. Once it laid the lines of segregation bare. For years, only the largely white sports – rugby, cricket, golf – received necessary funds for development.

Great strides have been made since South Africa's readmission to the international arena. In a spirit of reconciliation, Nelson Mandela donned a Springbok jersey following their victory in the 1995 rugby World Cup final. Soccer is big among the black population, and the national team lifted the African Nations Cup trophy in 1996, reaching the World Cup finals in 1998 and 2002. All South African sporting bodies have tried to create a more equal sporting society. The United Cricket Board set up an impressive development programme in the townships and rural areas. South Africa hosted both the 2010 FIFA World Cup and the 2013 Africa Cup of Nations, both telling indicators of the country's rising stock on the international sports scene.

popular spectator sports include boxing, wrestling and athletics.

SHOPPING

South Africa's shops are remarkably diverse—from flea markets and quaint bazaars to air-conditioned boutiques and big-city shopping malls vast enough for hours of browsing.

Visitors buying more expensive items, or a lot of cheaper ones, can reclaim the value-added tax (VAT) at their point

Arts and crafts for sale

of departure from the country. To do so they must show the items concerned as well as proper VAT receipts.

With its rich mix of cultures, South Africa has an abundance of artists and craftsmen, including painters and sculptors, glass-blowers, jewellery-makers, furniture-makers, and weavers and spinners, who produce hand-knitted garments and painted fabrics. Arts and crafts routes enable visitors to see the artists and view their work in their studios. Ask the local tourist association for details and maps regarding arts and crafts routes and markets in the area you're visiting.

When considering a purchase of arts or crafts, ask about the item's provenance. Old (antique) South African beadwork and San (Bushman) curios are very rare.

WHAT TO BUY

African curios. There's no end to the supply of tribal shields, spears and masks, most of which are produced by the manual equivalent of assembly lines. Some of the more artistic

Ivory ban

Most countries now ban imports of ivory in order to prevent the poaching of elephants. This ban also applies to elephant tusks that result from the legitimate, controlled hunting of elephants in Kruger National Park.

designs and older items come from other countries, in particular the Democratic Republic of Congo, Ghana and Côte d'Ivoire.

Beads. Early traders from Europe brought glass beads to exchange for ivory or other valuable commodities. Now European tourists buy beadwork necklaces and ornaments in various bright geometric designs.

Chess sets. Figurines of African warriors represent the pawns, medicine men the bishops, and so on.

Diamonds. Jewellers licensed by the South African customs give duty-free preference to bona-fide foreign visitors on diamonds that are cut, ground and polished but not set. Semi-precious stones, which also abound here, come closer to most budgets: these include agate, amethyst, jasper, rose quartz and verdite.

Indian spices. Curry powders and chilli peppers with explosive colours and flavours are fitting souvenirs of Durban.

Jewellery. Certain jewellers with special customs licences are able to sell gold pendants, chains and earrings to visitors without charging the stiff levels of South African duty. You will have to show your passport, air ticket and flight reservation to qualify.

Krugerrands. Collectors of gold will always be pleased to receive one, or a set, of these desirable and portable South African coins. They may be purchased duty-free for foreign currency in the departure lounge of Johannesburg's Jan Smuts Airport.

Musical instruments. You will soon learn to play one of those small bush xylophones with metal spikes and a carved wooden base. You can also take home a small drum-rattle or a big carved drum to thump.

Pottery. African artisans produce coiled pots with ancient tribal designs or thrown pots with original motifs.

Rugs and tapestries. Handwoven in geometric or figurative designs, these are suitable for wall-hangings or carpets. From spinning wheel to final trimming, some of these works of rural art are produced with meticulous care.

Seashells and coral. Those vast beaches turn up seashells which serious collectors covet. Coral fantasies, although controversial, are sold in curio shops on the coast and inland.

Straw goods. Bags, baskets, hats, mats and trays are often sold in souvenir shops or by the roadside at makeshift stalls.

Tanzanite jewellery on show

Wines. Quality wines and local versions of sherries, ports and brandies make natural souvenirs of the Cape (see pages 81 and 102).

Woodcraft. Salad bowls, meat trays, spoons and ladles are readily available. Wooden sculptures run from miniature rhinos to large, elaborate carvings incorporating entire tribes of figures. The fine-grained local hardwoods make solid furniture and fine carvings. Don't be put off by the name given to stinkwood–it only smells when freshly cut.

African penguins, Boulders Beach

ENTERTAINMENT

In Johannesburg, Melville and the revitalised Braamfontein are now the most popular areas to go for live music, restaurants, and **clubs**. For details of the latest venues, and events, consult the local press or the weekly *Mail & Guardian* newspaper.

In the major cities, **theatres** present plays in either English or Afrikaans. Some of the most important include the State Theatre in Pretoria (www.statetheatre.co.za), Joburg Theatre (www.joburgtheatre.com) and Cape Town's Baxter Theatre (www.baxter.co.za). The Johannesburg Festival Orchestra (http://jfo.co.za) performs in the major centres and there are a number of accomplished opera and ballet companies.

Cinemas show current international film releases, and the high level of censorship associated with the apartheid era has been greatly relaxed.

In larger towns and cities, tickets to films, plays and concerts may be bought at *Computicket* stores, a computerised booking agency (tel: 083-915 8000, http://online.computicket.com).

CHILDREN'S SOUTH AFRICA

South Africa is very welcoming to children and you will find plenty of entertainment on offer, especially in summer. The large choice of self-catering accommodation makes it easy to accommodate the needs of children of different ages.

In **Cape Town** most children are thrilled by the ride to the top of Table Mountain. Older children should find a trip to Robben Island thought-provoking and moving. The South African Museum has exhibits geared towards children, and the adjoining Planetarium offers regular children's shows. At the V&A Waterfront, kids will love the Two Oceans Aquarium. The penguins at Boulders Beach are amazing for the whole family, and even the most blasé teenager cannot help but be impressed by the majestic sight of whales at Hermanus.

Child-friendly attractions in the **Winelands** include the Spier Wine Estate south of Stellenbosch which has kids' programmes in summer and a cheetah park.

In **Johannesburg** are a zoo and Gold Reef City, where you can tour an authentic gold mine as well as enjoy a variety of thrilling rides. **Pretoria** Zoo is world-renowned, and at the Sun City resort there are kids' clubs and a water park.

Durban's Natural Science Museum is small but fascinating, and uShaka Marine World (www.ushakamarineworld.co.za) has a shark dive tank as well as daily shows featuring seals, dolphins and penguins.

Port Elizabeth has a wide range of safe, well-maintained beaches, and just outside is **Addo National Park**, where you can go on self-drive tours and see elephants.

Many of the game reserves dotted around the country will have children's facilities, such as playrooms, special game drives, babysitting and kids' meals earlier in the evening.

CALENDAR OF EVENTS

January *Cape Minstrels Carnival*, Cape Town.

February *Dance Umbrella – a festival of choreography and dance*, Johannesburg, Gauteng.

March *Cape Town International Jazz Festival, Lambert's Bay Kreeffees – crayfish feast in Lambert's Bay, West Coast, Western Cape*.

March–April *Klein Karoo National Arts Festival*, Oudtshoorn – week-long festival featuring music, drama and dance. *Rand Show* (two weeks around Easter), Johannesburg – the largest trade exposition in South Africa, Scifest Africa – a seven-day national science festival featuring lectures, workshops and much more, Grahamstown, Eastern Cape.

April *Music in the Mountains Festival*, Drakensberg Boys School, Kwa-Zulu-Natal. *Old Mutual Two Oceans Marathon*, Cape Town. *Tulbagh Goes Dutch Festival* – celebrations of the town's Cape Dutch heritage, Afri-caBurn – South Africa's answer to the Burning Man in Tankwa Karoo.

May *Cape Gourmet Festival*, Cape Town – two-week event held across the city. *Rooms on View International Decor Fair*, Sandton, Gauteng.

May–June *Comrades Marathon*, KwaZulu-Natal – gruelling marathon, held in either Durban or Pietermaritzburg.

June *National Arts Festival*, Grahamstown, Eastern Cape – a fortnight of drama, dance, visual arts, music and film.

July *Biltong Festival*, Somerset East, Eastern Cape – Afrikaner country festival. *Hibiscus Festival*, South Coast, KwaZulu-Natal. *Durban International Film Festival*, University of Natal, Durban.

August *Hermanus Wine and Food Fair*, Western Cape.

August–September *Pretoria Show* – long running agricultural show.

September *Arts Alive*, various venues, Johannesburg – month-long celebration of the performing arts. *North-West Cultural Calabash*, Taung – recommended African arts festival. *Whale Festival*, Hermanus, Western Cape. *Jeffrey's Bay Shell Festival*, Eastern Cape.

October *Food and Wine Festival*, Stellenbosch, Western Cape. *Jacaranda Festival*, Market Square, Pretoria.

November *Cherry Festival*, Ficksburg, Free State.

December *Rustler's Valley New Year Celebration*, Ficksburg, Free State.

EATING OUT

With 13 million head of cattle on South African ranchland and two oceans to provide the fish, you're assured of good food in abundance. Cooking here has the old-fashioned virtues – it's wholesome and there's plenty of it. You may indeed be daunted by the sizes of the portions. In many restaurants 'doggy bags' are called for, in the American way, so that the excess can be taken home.

City restaurants come in all varieties, from five-star haute cuisine and elegance down to the most utilitarian fast-food joint. Italian, French, Chinese and Portuguese/Mozambican cuisines abound, but Johannesburg claims ethnic restaurants of 20 nationalities, including Japanese, Korean, Greek, Indonesian, Turkish and Mexican. Many Cape restaurants serve old Cape Dutch and Malay recipes. Durban is noted for its Indian restaurants, and offers the cuisines of various regions of that continent.

The braaivleis is part of the South African way of life

In South Africa, the term café is conventionally applied to a small store similar in nature to the British corner shop. Cafés of this sort often serve cheap greasy take-away food and soft drinks, but will have nowhere to sit down and eat. In cities, however, the more familiar sit-down café has become an increasingly commonplace feature of post-apartheid South Africa, in particular the popular Vida e Caffè chain.

In all hotels except, paradoxically, the most expensive, breakfast will normally be included in the price. Even if it isn't, it's likely to be good value, typically consisting of fresh fruit and juice, hot or cold cereals, bacon or sausage, eggs, toast and rolls, butter and marmalade and tea or coffee. Many hotels have breakfast buffets in the Scandinavian manner, though the dishes on offer are more British in derivation, as is the morning 'wake-up' coffee or tea that you can have brought to your room.

Traditional South African dishes at the Gold Restaurant, Cape Town

At the game lodges it makes sense to take that coffee or tea at dawn or before, then go out looking for the wildlife prior to returning for a hearty mid-morning breakfast or brunch.

FISH AND SEAFOOD

All along the coast you'll find fish restaurants that clearly have good connections down at the harbour.

But the majority of restaurants, specialist or not, have fish on the menu –and usually fresh. Cape salmon is a tasty white fish, unrelated to the salmon of Europe and North America. *Kabeljou* is similar to cod. *Kingklip*, a large meaty fish, makes fine fillets. *Snoek*, a cold-water fish about a yard long, is served smoked as a starter or grilled as a main course, while *Steenbras* resembles sea bream.

Food festivals

You might wish to consider timing your visit to South Africa to coincide with a food festival, such as the South African Cheese Festival held at Paarl from late April to early May, www.cheese festival.co.za, the Good Food & Wine Show held at Cape Town in late May, http://capetown.goodfood andwineshow.co.za, or early July's Knysna Oyster Festival, www.oysterfestival.co.za.

The excellent shellfish is worth seeking out: mussels, *perlemoen* (abalone), prawns (the latter often imported from Mozambique). The local crayfish (elsewhere called spiny rock lobster) is a delicacy. Oysters may be served with hot sauce already applied–remember to specify in advance if you want yours unadulterated.

MEAT

South Africa's favourite food is *braaivleis* (barbecued meat), a feast cooked in the garden or at a picnic spot. Men are generally in charge and the whole business is taken seriously: special cuts of meat are sold for the purpose, and hardwood is selected for its proper fire-making qualities.

You may be invited to a *braai* (see box) or you can buy the meats and the wood and use the barbecue you'll find outside most chalets or rondavels in game park camps. Otherwise, the many steak houses serve a pretty good approximation of the outdoor taste. The steaks–fillet, rump, sirloin, tournedos, or T-bone—are invariably big, thick and tender. Whether you ask for it or not, the cook is liable to grill them with a barbecue sauce. A number of other sauces are usually on the menu, the most piquant being 'monkey gland' sauce (hot sauce and chutney).

In steak houses and other restaurants you'll also find a variety of alternatives: lamb, veal, pork, poultry and game. All dishes come with potatoes (usually chips—French fries— or baked) or, less commonly, rice and cooked vegetables—beans, broccoli, carrots, mushrooms, pumpkin, squash, sweet potatoes or *mealies* (corn on the cob). Steak houses and some other restaurants may have salad bars in the American style—a big choice of nutritious raw vegetables and dressings to mix and match.

LOCAL FAVOURITES

Don't miss the traditional South African meat dishes, particularly *bobotie*, a baked minced-meat recipe from the Cape. It's probably of Malay origin, with its additions of apricot, almond,

BRAAI

If you can eat it, you can *braai* it. Originally an Afrikaner social tradition, the barbecueing of large quantities of meat and any other food to hand is something of a national institution in South Africa. Each weekend, wood fires are lit in countless gardens for the family *braaivleis* (in Afrikaans *braai* means to grill, *vleis* means meat).

The most popular foods to barbecue are lamb chops, curried *sosaties* (skewered meat), *boerewors* (spicy beef or pork sausages), *biltong* (dry, salted meat) and freshly picked corn on the cob. The secret of a good *braai* is to cook the meat as slowly as possible while keeping it moist with marinade.

Boerewors (dried sausages) are a popular local snack

chutney, and a subtle spicing of curry. *Boerewors* is a flavour-ful country sausage, usually of a beef and pork combination. *Bredie* is a rich ragout, usually of mutton, with a thick tomato sauce. *Sosaties* are kebabs, resembling Southeast Asia's *satés*, little pieces of lamb marinated in vinegar, sugar, gar-lic, curry powder and apricot. Varieties of smoked pork are another local speciality.

Biltong, strips of dried meat, was once made out of neces-sity, to take on treks and for preserving surplus meat before the days of refrigeration. Now it's something of a delicacy. *Biltong* is most often made with beef, but game *biltong* – from various antelopes and ostrich – is also widely available.

DESSERTS

If you have space, there may be apple pie, *melktert* (minimal pastry and a light, gently spiced custard), cheesecake, or trifle in the English style (sponge cake smothered in fruit, nuts, custard and whipped cream). Then, of course, there's always

Huguenot cuisine

The arrival of the Huguenots in 1688 brought a French influence to South African cuisine. Settling in the Franschhoek valley, they harvested fruit and produced wine. The Afrikaans term for fruit preserves and jams, *konfyt*, comes from the French technique for preserving food by long, slow simmering – *confit*.

fresh fruit—small, sweet pineapples, bananas of various kinds, melons, apples, grapes and *naartjies* (mandarin oranges). Also, look out for home-made ice-cream with real fruit flavours.

South African versions of many European cheeses – including brie, camembert, cheddar, gouda, mozzarella and so on—lack the quality of the European originals, but their price is lower. Parmesan is expensive.

Before you've finished your dessert the waiter may present you with the bill. This is not intended to hurry you out. Nevertheless, it is rare for South Africans to linger at the table after a meal.

WINE AND OTHER DRINKS

Cape wines have come a long way. The early settlers grew the classic grape varieties, but the same plague that ravaged the vines in Europe in the 1880s also struck South Africa, and the country's vineyards had to be replanted with resistant American grafts.

Today, the most widely planted white grape is Chenin Blanc, sometimes known locally as Steen, and used to make anything from bone dry whites to brandy. Other popular white varieties include Chardonnay, Sauvignon Blanc and Colombar (the latter used mostly for dessert and brandy). Common red varieties include Cabernet Sauvignon, Merlot, Syrah (normally referred to as Shiraz in South Africa) and Pinotage, a cross between Pinot Noir and Cinsaut (Hermitage) pioneered in the Cape in the 1920s (see page 81).

Aside from wine, there are lager-style beers (served very cold), well-known brands of soft drinks (called cool drinks) and mineral waters. Fruit juices, freshly squeezed or pasteurised, are delicious. Look out for some of the exotic mixtures: guava, lime, mango, apricot, peach and pear. You won't cause any surprise by asking for tap water, which is drinkable everywhere.

Bear in mind that some restaurants lack wine or liquor licences, especially in Cape Town, so it is wise to check in advance. Note that a corkage charge of R20–80 may be applicable. South Africans often bring their own wine to licence less restaurants. If you don't, it's no good expecting to go to a nearby wine shop: they open only during normal shopping hours and never on Sunday.

Wine is very popular in South Africa

PLACES TO EAT

We have used the following symbols to give an idea of the price for a three-course meal for one, not including drinks:

$$$** over R250   **$$** R120–250   **$ up to R120

JOHANNESBURG AND ENVIRONS

Les Delices De France $$$ *corner Gordon Road and Keith Ave, Roodepoort, tel: 11 027 8668,* http://lesdelicesdefrance.co.za. Authentic French cuisine served in a modern environment; made exclusively from the highest quality produce. Lovely patio and garden make this the perfect place for al fresco dining. Friendly atmosphere and welcoming French owners. Closed on Mondays.

The Carnivore $$$ *Muldersdrift Estate, Muldersdrift, tel: 011-950 6000;* www.rali.co.za. This South African branch of its legendary Nairobi namesake is renowned for its vast all-you-can-eat buffet, which consists of 15 different types of (mostly game) meat spit-roasted over a huge charcoal fire in the middle of the restaurant. As well as the usual lamb, beef and pork, the restaurant offers venison, crocodile, wildebeest and many others.

Moyo Melrose Arch $$ *The High Street, Shop 5, Melrose Arch, tel: 011 684 1477;* www.moyo.co.za. Located in the heart of Johannes-burg, this multi-level modern restaurant offers authentic South African cuisine and live music. Specialities include a great vari-ety of starters such as fried mopane worms, springbok carpaccio or peri peri chicken. There are also large grilled meat dishes for groups to share.

Osteria Tre Nonni $$ *9 Grafton Avenue, Craighall Park, tel: 0861-222 532.* This friendly restaurant is always abuzz with Italian families tucking into authentic dishes straight out of Tuscany and Umbria.

Trumps Grillhouse and Butchery $$$ *Shop 11, Nelson Mandela Square, Sandton, tel: 011 784 2366,* www.trumpsgrill.co.za. Once a modest, family-owned restaurant, Trumps reopened in mid-2015 as a stylish grillhouse, boasting a modern interior with an in-store butchery and an extensive wine and whiskey cellar. Finest quality, grain-fed Karan beef and lamb make the perfect base for the traditional South African braai. The meat is so tender it will melt in your mouth. Besides T-Bones, sirloins, ribeyes and lamb loins, the restaurant also offers vegetarian dishes including halloumi and falafel burgers as well as salads and seafood. Open daily 11.30am–11pm.

PRETORIA

Café Riche $–$$ *Church Square, tel: 012-328 3173.* Open from 6am until after midnight, this stalwart people-watching and one-last-nightcap venue lies on the corner of historic Church Square, smack in the middle of the city centre. Their extensive selection of cakes, croissants, salads and snacks is supplemented with tasty meals, usually with a distinctive South African flavour.

La Madeleine $$$ *122 Priory Road, Lynnwood, Pretoria, tel: 012-361 3667, www.lamadeleine.co.za.* Sensational Provençal food. Simplicity is the watchword of Daniel Leusch's cooking, and it's won him many laurels. Open for dinner Tuesday to Saturday and for brunch on Sundays.

DURBAN AND ENVIRONS

Bombay 2 Beirut $$ *237 O.R. Tambo Parade (Marine Parade), Point Waterfront, Durban, tel: 031-332 1786.* Good Indian cuisine supplemented by an array of Lebanese, Chinese and other exotic dishes.

Butcher Boys $$$ *170 Florida Road, Morningside, tel: 031-312 8248; http://butcherboysgrill.co.za.* As the name suggests, an excellent venue for steaks and other meat dishes.

Cargo Hold $$ *uShaka Marine World, Point Waterfront, tel: 031-328 8065; www.ushakamarineworld.co.za.* International menu in a mock shipwreck overlooked by the shark tank of Durban's famous aquarium (see page 52).

Golden Chopsticks $ *Belmont Arcade, City Centre, tel: 031-332 8970.* Popular waterfront restaurant that has been serving top-notch Cantonese food for three full decades.

Harvey's $$$ *465 Innes Road, Morningside, tel: 031-312 5706; www. harveysrestaurant.co.za.* Stylish, modern, award-winning restaurant with cutting-edge dishes. Busy and popular all the time.

Indian Connection $$ *485 Windermere Road, Morningside, tel: 031-312 1440.* There is no shortage of excellent Indian eateries in Durban, and this is one of the best, with a varied menu of spicy dishes catering to devoted carnivores and seafood lovers, as well as to vegetarians.

Oyster Bar & Zenbi Sushi $$–$$$ *14 Boatman's Road, Wilson's Wharf, tel: 031-307 7883.* Offering a great view of Durban's harbour, this stylish restaurant is known for its fresh seafood, which includes line fish, prawns by the kilo, succulent oysters and fine sushi – to be washed down with a crisp white from the excellent wine list. Closed Monday.

Roma Revolving Restaurant $$ *32nd floor, John Street House, Margaret Mncadi Avenue (Victoria Embankment), Durban, tel: 031-368 2275, www.roma.co.za.* In business since 1973, this slowly revolving restaurant affords spectacular views of the city and harbour. Classic Italian dishes are served up in a plush, comfortable interior. The champagne sole is hard to beat. Closed on Sundays.

Ulundi $$$ *The Royal Hotel, 247 Anton Lembede Street (Smith Street), Durban, tel: 082-040 5887, www.ulundi-restaurant.co.za.* This is another renowned curry restaurant set in the splendidly time-warped colonial-style surroundings of The Royal Hotel (see page 136).

PORT ELIZABETH

Blue Waters Café $$ *Hobie Beach, Port Elizabeth, tel: 041-583 4110, www.bluewaterscafe.com.* Popular with locals, this place offers good service and outside seating on a terrace overlooking the sea. They don't cater very well for vegetarians, but there is a good selection of burgers, steaks, pasta, fish and chicken. A good spot for sundowners and afternoon coffee too.

Ginger Restaurant $$ *Marine Drive, Summerstrand, Port Elizabeth, tel: 041-583 1229,* www.ginger-restaurant.co.za. Subtle dishes with an Eastern Cape influence make for a fine dining experience. Generous portions, good wine list and a modern, spacious interior with outside verandah. Lighter lunch menu.

CAPE TOWN AND ENVIRONS

Africa Café $$ *108 Shortmarket Street, Heritage Square, tel: 021-422 0221,* www.africacafe.co.za. This popular vegetarian-friendly eatery offers a wide selection of dishes originating from the Cape to Cairo and most places in-between, all served in lively, vibrant surroundings.

Biesmiellah $ *Upper Wale Street, Bo-Kaap, Cape Town, tel: 021-23 0850.* This well-established and authentic-feeling eatery in the old Malay quarter serves a selection of spicy traditional Cape Malay dishes. The food is halal and no alcohol is served. Closed on Sundays.

Blues $$$ *The Promenade, Victoria Road, Camps Bay, tel: 021-438 2040;* www.blues.co.za. Californian-style cuisine served in a spacious, airy room overlooking one of the world's most pristinely beautiful beaches. It's always packed, and very pricey, so book well ahead and carry a credit card.

Boschendal Restaurant $$ *Groot Drakenstein, tel: 021-870 4274;* www.boschendal.com. Situated on the wine estate of the same name between Stellenbosch and Franschhoek, this restaurant offers first-class South African cuisine in elegant surroundings, and is also well-known for its affordable picnic lunches, which can be eaten on the beautiful lawns.

Bread & Wine $$ *Môreson Farm, Happy Valley Road, Franschhoek, tel: 021-876 3692;* www.moreson.co.za. This well-regarded rustic restaurant serves up excellent cheese and charcuterie plates as well as more substantial mains. There is also a deli where you can stock up on pickles, preserves, sausages and hams.

Buitenverwachting $$ *Klein Constantia Road, Constantia, tel: 021-794 3522;* www.buitenverwachting.com. The name means 'beyond expectation' and that's a fair description of this wonderful restaurant set on a stunning wine estate. Impressive wine list. Closed Monday and during August.

Cape Malay Restaurant $$ *The Cellars-Hohenort Hotel, 93 Brommersvlei Road, Constantia, tel: 021-794 2137.* Traditional Cape Malay restaurant in this luxury hotel (see page 138). Best of the country's indigenous cuisine.

Constantia Nek $$ *Hout Bay Road, Constantia Nek, tel: 021-794 5132;* www.constantianek.co.za. Between Hout Bay and Constantia. Set close to the main wine estates on the Cape Peninsula, this stalwart serves a good selection of a la carte dishes during the week, and is well-known for its all-you-can-eat Sunday carvery. Closed on Mondays.

Constantia Uitsig $$$ *Spaanschemat River Road, Constantia, tel: 021-794 4480.* This wine farm restaurant offers fine Provençal cooking where fish and game are specialities. The spectacular mountainous setting, a short drive south of central Cape Town, matches the superb food.

Green Dolphin $$ *Victoria & Alfred Arcade, Cape Town, tel: 021-421 7471.* Boasting a great location on the redeveloped dockside Victoria & Alfred Waterfront, this legendary pub is best known for the live jazz bands that play in the evening, but it's also a fine sundowner venue and serves a good selection of seafood, pasta, pizza and Cape wines.

Île de Pain $ *Unit 10, The Boatshed, Thesen Harbour Town, Knysna, tel: 044-302 5707,* www.iledepain.co.za. This fabulous bakery is a local institution, famous along the Garden Route. As well as great breads, pastries and croissants, the accompanying menu features dishes like duck confit and steak with rocket and parmesan. Try the delectable hot chocolate.

JB Rivers Café and Cocktail Saloon $$ *Cavendish Square, Cape Town, tel: 021-683 0840.* This restaurant offers New Orleans-style spicy Cajun cooking, as well as a good range of steaks, seafood, salads and even a sushi bar with a highly experienced sushi chef – not to mention a multitude of intriguing cocktails.

Tapas and Oysters $ *H 29, Thesen Island, Knysna, tel: 044-382 7196; www.tapasknysna.co.za.* Cheap-and-cheerful joint serving tapas, oysters cultivated in Knysna lagoon, and the local draught beer.

Morton's on the Wharf $$ *Shop 221, Victoria Wharf, Victoria & Alfred Waterfront, tel: 021-418 3633.* One of the best bars and restaurants crowding this thriving dock-side complex. Cajun and Creole cooking.

Panama Jack's $$ *Royal Yacht Club Basin, off Goliath Road, Dockside, tel: 021-447 3992; www.panamajacks.net.* Fabulous fresh seafood dishes in friendly, informal surroundings.

Le Quartier Français $$$ *16 Huguenot Street, Franschhoek, tel: 021-876 2151.* Cuisine reflecting influences of the region's original French settler families, set in the historic heart of the scenic Franschhoek Valley.

The Savoy Cabbage $$$ *Heritage Square, 101 Hout Street, tel: 021-424 2626; www.savoycabbage.co.za.* Hearty food, sometimes in odd combinations, with notable local influence. The city-centre building is an interesting blend of old and new. Closed Sunday.

A–Z TRAVEL TIPS

A Summary of Practical Information

A

ACCOMMODATION (see also Camping, Youth Hostels and Recommended Hotels)

The South African Tourism board (www.tourismgrading.co.za) publishes a directory of hotels with ratings. The prices match the standards, but the degree of comfort of hotels at the lower end of the scale is also notable. Many two-star establishments, for instance, have spacious air-conditioned rooms, and one-star hotels have a high percentage of rooms with private baths.

The directory also includes luxury lodges and rest camps in game parks, beach cottages, holiday flats, and caravan and campsites, and can be obtained, or ordered, from South African Tourism's national and international offices (see page 127); it is invaluable for planning ahead, for use on arrival, and while you're touring. In resort areas, mid-range and family-orientated accommodation catering mostly or partially to the local leisure market is normally heavily booked over South African school holiday periods (December to January, Easter, June to July and early October). By contrast, city hotels catering mostly to the local business market are typically busy on Monday to Thursday nights and are quieter over the weekend, when discounted rates may be available. Up-market accommodation and backpacker hostels servicing the international market tend to be busiest during the main inbound tourist season, which generally runs from September to May. At other times, reduced off-season prices may apply. Self-catering apartments, along with bed and breakfast, have become increasingly popular in South Africa as they offer an economically viable alternative to expensive hotels.

Among many other details, the directory reports the status of every establishment's alcohol licence (if any), its policy on pets, whether there is wheelchair access, and gives an indication of price. Prices include VAT at the standard rate.

AIRPORTS

O.R. Tambo International Airport is about 24km (15 miles) from central Johannesburg and 60km (37 miles) from Pretoria. For airport enquiries tel: 011-921 6262 or 086-727 7888.

An increasing number of international flights touch down at the Durban and Cape Town international airports. **King Shaka International Airport** (tel: 032 436 6000 or 086 727 7888), which opened in 2010, is located 30km (19 miles) north of Durban. **Cape Town Airport** (tel: 021-937 1200) is 22km (14 miles) southeast of the city.

Most upmarket hotels now offer airport shuttles to pre-booked clients, often at no additional charge. Metered taxis are available at all airports, and private shuttles can be arranged through a company called Airport Shuttle, www.airportshuttle.co.za. Gautrain (www.gautrain.co.za) links Pretoria with Johannesburg, Ekhuruleni and O.R Tambo International Airport. It operates daily from 5.15am to 10pm, with services approximately every 12 minutes.

Domestic routes flown by South African Airways and a number of small independent airlines link the main cities and some smaller centres. If you are going to Kruger National Park, SAA flies to **Kruger Mpumalanga Airport** (tel: 013-753 7500, www.kmiairport.co.za), from which you can get a transfer to your game lodge. Private airlines operate flights to other towns and to Skukuza and Phalaborwa, also serving Kruger. For enquiries relating to SAA flights, tel: 0861 FLYSAA or 0861 606 606 or see www.flysaa.com. For further information about airports, visit www.airports.co.za.

B

BUDGETING FOR YOUR TRIP

The following is an approximate guide to prices in South Africa.
Airport transfers. Taxi from O.R. Tambo International Airport to central Johannesburg costs from R230 upwards; taxi from Cape Town International Airport to central Cape Town: R230.

Excursions. Full-day Cape Peninsula tour from Cape Town: R900–950; three-day Johannesburg–Kruger Park coach tour including most meals, entry fees and accommodation (shared room, per person): R8,000; full-day Johannesburg–Sun City coach tour including Pilanesberg game drive: from R2000 per person.

Flights. Flights from the UK to South Africa are around £600–800, and more expensive at Christmas. Emirates usually offer cheap flights, but include a stopover in Dubai. The journey from Johannesburg to Cape Town costs around R1,400–2,000.

Hairdressers. Man's haircut: R180–200 (tip expected); woman's haircut, shampoo, set and blow-dry: R300–400 (tip expected).

Hotels (double room with bath). 5-star: from R3,500 upwards, 3-star: R800+ with breakfast, 1-star: R550+ with breakfast.

Meals and drinks (medium-priced restaurant). Lunch: R100; dinner: R100–200; bottle of wine: R80 upward; beer: R–24; liquor R24 upward; soft drink: R10–15.

Museums. R10–230.

National Parks. Entry fees: R80–230 per adult, 50 percent less per child (under 12). Campsites: from R225. Check the SANParks website for current tariffs: www.sanparks.org.

Petrol. R12.78 per litre.

Trains (one way). Johannesburg–Cape Town, normal train: from R690; Blue Train, standard compartment (per person, meals included): from R18,000 upwards. Johannesburg–Pretoria: R30; Johannesburg–Durban: R330.

C

CAMPING

Good weather and good roads account for the popularity of camping and caravanning in South Africa. There are about 650 caravan parks around the country, often in beautiful surroundings. Many have tent sites and amenities for campers too. Facilities at most sites are relatively lavish. Popular parks, especially near the beaches, are likely to be full from mid-December to mid-January and at Easter. A good website for campsites is www.sa-venues.com.

You can rent a fully equipped caravan and the car to tow it, or, less widely available, a self-contained motor caravan (camper).

CAR HIRE (See also Driving and Budgeting for Your Trip)

Some well-known international and local car-hire firms have offices at airports, in all big cities and even small towns throughout South Africa. The local companies usually have slightly lower tariffs. You need a valid driver's licence and usually a minimum age (23 or 25) is specified. A cash deposit may be required unless a recognised credit card is used for payment. A VW Polo will cost R400–500 per day; a minibus (VW Caravelle) R1,000–1,200 per day. Rates include basic insurance and sometimes collision damage waiver and personal accident insurance as well. Prices are generally cheaper the longer the duration of hire. There may be a per-kilometre charge. Fuel is not included. Rates will usually be lower if you reserve a car before arriving in South Africa, perhaps as part of a package booked through a travel agent. Chauffeur-driven cars are also available. As a rule, hire cars may not cross South Africa's borders. Car hire companies include:

Avis, tel: 0861-021 111, www.avis.co.za

Budget, tel: 0861-016 622, www.budget.co.za

Europ Car, tel: 0861-131 000, www.europcar.co.za

Hertz, tel: 0861-600 136, www.hertz.co.za

Thrifty, tel: 0861-002 111, www.thrifty.co.za

CLIMATE

Arriving from the northern hemisphere, the seasons are reversed south of the equator: July is mid-winter and Christmas can be hot. Winter nights can be cold, especially at higher altitudes–and that includes Johannesburg –though daytime temperatures are often delightful. In the parks and reserves game-spotting is easiest in winter (from July to October). Because it's dry then, there's much less foliage to afford cover to the animals. However, winter in Cape Town can be rainy.

	J	F	M	A	M	J	J	A	S	O	N	D
Cape Town												
°C max	26	27	26	23	20	18	17	18	19	21	24	25
°F max	79	80	79	74	68	64	63	64	66	70	75	77
°C min	16	16	15	13	11	9	8	9	10	12	14	15
°F min	61	61	59	55	52	48	46	48	50	54	57	59
Johannesburg												
°C max	26	26	24	22	19	16	16	20	23	25	25	26
°F max	79	79	75	72	66	61	61	68	74	77	77	79
°C min	14	13	13	10	7	4	4	6	9	12	13	14
°F min	57	55	55	50	45	39	39	43	48	54	55	57

CLOTHING

Even in summer, a degree of formality is appropriate after dark in smarter hotels. Otherwise, South Africans are very casual: jeans, sandals and even shorts are acceptable for men.

At holiday resorts and while you're in transit, very casual clothing suffices. Fancy safari suits are quite unnecessary in the game parks; anything comfortable will do, though darker colours seem to attract fewer insects.

For South African summers, pack lightweight clothing, and a light jacket or sweater for the occasional chilly evening. A raincoat or umbrella also would be useful; summer is the rainy season in much of the country, though generally it's a matter of a passing thunderstorm to relieve the heat. (An exception is the Mediterranean-style Western Cape, which is dry all summer with rain in the winter.) On the Natal coast the Indian Ocean is swimmable all the year round.

CRIME AND SAFETY

As in much of the rest of the world, burglaries and muggings are commonplace in South African cities. Be prepared to find steel security gates and guards at restaurants, shops and car parks. Take the same precautions as at home and discuss any concerns with your hotel. If you are a victim of crime, report it at your nearest police station. You will need to produce identification. The police will give you a case reference number should you need to make an insurance claim. Do not wander after dark or go to townships alone.

D

DRIVING

With 73,500km (46,300 miles) of paved road, much of it excellent, South Africa is well suited for touring by car. Many of the national roads are tolled, so be sure to carry cash with you. Away from the cities, traffic is light and you can keep up high average speeds. Even dirt roads to more remote destinations are usually well graded.

Paperwork. You must have a valid driving licence with the details printed in English, or an accompanying certificate of authenticity in English, or an international licence, obtained before arrival in South Africa. To hire a car, there are no unusual requirements (see page 114), but if you plan to import a car, advance planning and documentation are complicated. For details, consult the South Africa Tourism board (see page 127) or the Automobile Association of South Africa: tel: 086 100-0234; www.aa.co.za.

Driving conditions. As part of the British legacy, South Africa drives on the left. The speed limit on main highways is 120km/h (75mph). Elsewhere, the indicated limit may be 100km/h (62mph) or 80km/h (50mph) and you are generally restricted to 60km/h (37mph) in built-up areas unless otherwise posted. Driving standards are variable and the accident rate is high. Many vehicles are not roadworthy, and speeding and drink-driving are common. In rural areas watch out for animals and pedestrians on the roads.

Police patrol cars are seen mostly near the cities and towns; if you break the law, you may be fined on the spot.

Road signs. Standard international pictographs are used for most situations, but there are some South African peculiarities. Printed signs are bilingual, for example, 'Border/Grens' or 'Ompad/Detour', or they alternate, so remember that Kaapstad means Cape Town. The frequently seen 'Slegs Only' with an arrow merely means the lane in question must only be used for turning. (*Slegs* means 'only' in Afrikaans.)

Parking restrictions are indicated by letters in circles painted on the road surface. Parking meters in most city centres have been replaced by uniformed staff – pay them directly.

'L' means loading zone (goods vehicles only); 'B' means reserved for buses, 'T' for taxis and 'FB' for fire-fighting equipment. 'S' with a diagonal stripe means no stopping, a striped 'P' is a no-parking indicator. Traffic lights are called 'robots' in English and Afrikaans.

Fuel. Filling stations are found on all main roads, although in country areas they're widely dispersed. Most filling stations are open 24 hours, seven days a week, but some stations in smaller towns may keep shorter hours, for instance from 7am until midnight. Most filling stations sell diesel, lead-free fuel and the recently introduced lead-replacement fuel (LRP) for vehicles that don't use lead-free.

Driving in the game parks and reserves. The Kruger National Park in particular is geared to the motor car, with about 900km (558 miles) of tarred roads, plus 1,500km (930 miles) of gravel roads. The speed limit is 50km/h (31mph) on tarred roads and 40km/h (25mph) on gravel, but slow driving gives animal pedestrians a better chance of survival, and you are more likely to sight game in the bush at 25km/h (15mph) – and on gravel or dirt roads you'll kick up much less dust.

Out of your car—even if you stick your head or arms out the window—you become a recognisable human, frightening some animals and prompting others to attack. Stay in the car anywhere beyond the fenced camps, barring an emergency. There are no tame animals, not even the lovable-looking vervet monkeys, which may bite. Feeding any animal is strictly forbidden.

Some more regulations: you may not drive off an authorised road into the bush or on to a road with a 'no entry' sign. Among other dangers, if your car should break down in an unauthorised place, help might not reach you for days. Any firearms must be declared and sealed at the gate. No pets are allowed.

One rule that is taken very seriously in the parks is the closing of the gates. In winter you must be back in your camp, or out of the park, by 5.30pm; in summer by 6.30pm. If you're late you'll be fined, even if the road was blocked by elephants.

Bookings for any of the country's 20 national parks can be made through www.sanparks.org, or through the SANParks head office in Pretoria (tel: 012-428 9111). Another important conservation body is KZN (KwaZulu-Natal) Wildlife, which manages 66 reserves in Zululand, the Drakensberg and elsewhere in the province – online bookings at www.kznwildlife.com or ring 033-845 1000/1999.

E

ELECTRICITY

Voltage is generally 220/230 volts AC, 50 cycles (but Pretoria's is 250V). Plugs have three round pins. Hardware stores and supermarkets sell adapters for electric razors and other appliances.

EMBASSIES AND CONSULATES

(See also the *Yellow Pages* of local telephone directories under Consulates and Embassies.)

Australia: Mutual and Federal Building, 292 Orient Street, Arcadia,

Pretoria; tel: 012-423 6000.
Canada: 1103 Arcadia Street, Hatfield, Pretoria; tel: 012-422 3000.
Ireland: 2nd Floor, Parkdev Building, Brooklyn Bridge Office Park, 570 Fehrsen Street, Pretoria, tel: 012 452 1000.
UK: 255 Hill Street, Arcadia, Pretoria; tel: 012-421 7500.
US: Thibault House, 877 Pretorius Street, Pretoria; tel: 012-431 4000. 2 Reddam Ave, Westlake 7945, Cape Town; tel: 021 702 7300

EMERGENCIES
Police: 10111
Ambulance: 10177
The National Tourism Information and Safety Line: 083 123 2345
From mobile phones:
All emergencies: 112
Fire Brigade: Johannesburg: 999, Cape Town: 535-1100, Durban: 361-0000
Information (electronic *Yellow Pages*) for all towns/cities: 10118

G

GAY AND LESBIAN TRAVELLERS
The self-proclaimed gay capital of South Africa, Cape Town is the most amenable city in Africa for gay visitors. The tourist department produces an official 'pink map' listing gay and lesbian orientated guesthouses, night venues and facilities, and there is a helpline operating daily (tel: 021-4222 500). A pink map is also produced for Johannesburg and Pretoria. The Pink Route is a collection of gay-owned lodges and hotels through the Western Cape.

GETTING THERE
Scheduled flights. You can fly to South Africa from North America direct and via a number of European cities, including Athens, London, Frankfurt, Lisbon, Paris, Rome and Zurich. There are non-stop flights

from London Heathrow to Johannesburg, where a connecting service is offered to Cape Town, Durban, Port Elizabeth and other South African cities. Several airlines also operate direct services to Cape Town and Durban. You may also fly via one of South Africa's neighbours, perhaps making a stopover on the way. Airlines that fly to South Africa include South African Airways (www.flysaa.com), British Airways (www.britishairways.com), Virgin Atlantic (www.virgin-atlantic.com), Emirates (www.emirates.com) and Air France (www.airfrance.com). The flight time from Europe is around 8–12 hours.

The months of January, July and December are peak season for fares. April and May fares are the lowest. Round the World (RTW) fares offered for certain routes include a stop in South Africa.

Charter flights and package tours

From North America: All-inclusive package tours are available. Costs covered include the round-trip airfare (usually from New York), accommodation, most or all meals, transfers, baggage handling, local transport and sightseeing.

From the UK: Tour operators offer a variety of holidays with everything included, as well as land-only packages if you wish to arrange your own air travel. Certain airlines can obtain hotel and car-hire discounts for their passengers. The South African Tourism board, (see page 127), gives information on tours and package holidays.

Some charter flights are currently offered to Johannesburg, but you must reserve far ahead as space fills up quickly.

GUIDES AND TOURS

City sightseeing tours and day excursions to beauty spots are normally led by bilingual (English and Afrikaans) guides. For interpreters of other languages, check with the local tourist office. Package tours of Kruger National Park are led by experienced guides who can help spot the animals and identify them for you. In the private game parks rangers are able to give their attention to visitors' individual interests.

H

HEALTH AND MEDICAL CARE

Vaccinations. No vaccinations are required for entry into South Africa unless you are arriving from a yellow-fever zone, in which case you must have an international yellow-fever vaccination certificate.

Malaria preventative tablets should be taken by everyone planning to visit the low veld of Mpumalanga or Limpopo Provinces (the Kruger Park or the private game parks nearby), Zululand in KwaZulu-Natal, or certain areas of South Africa's neighbours. Ask your pharmacist or doctor to explain the precautions you must take. Or you can go to any pharmacy in South Africa and buy anti-malaria pills over the counter. Normally, you must start taking the pills several days before entering the affected district and continue the specified dosage for several weeks after leaving. As an additional precaution, try to avoid being bitten by mosquitoes, one variety of which is responsible for spreading the disease. Apply an insect repellent, cover up your skin outdoors after dusk, and keep mosquitoes out of your sleeping area, by using mosquito netting and/or air-conditioning.

Other problems. Apart from 'bluebottles' (man-o-war jellyfish) and tides, swimming in the ocean presents no special problems. However, you should be extremely careful about rivers and lakes: unless otherwise indicated, they may be inhabited by the dangerous bilharzia parasite, which can be contracted by ingesting unpurified water or through bare feet or skin in or near the water. Never drink from a river unless you've been assured its water is safe to drink.

Most of the 140 varieties of snake in South Africa are harmless, or almost, but if the worst happens, anti-snakebite serum is available.

Beware of the power of the sun. You can feel cool by the sea, or at higher altitudes, and still burn yourself. Limit exposure and use a sunscreen with a protection factor of at least 15.

Insurance. Since South Africa has no national health service, any medical treatment and hospitalisation must be paid for direct. If you have medical insurance already, make certain that it covers foreign countries. Otherwise, take out special travel insurance that includes coverage of accidents, illness, or hospitalisation on your trip.

Doctors. Most hotels have a list of nearby doctors in case of need. Or look in the white pages of the telephone directory under 'Mediese Praktisyns' or 'Medical Practitioners'.

Hospitals. All cities have well-equipped hospitals.

Pharmacies. In the big cities one pharmacy in each area stays open after normal business hours. Check in the local newspaper or at your hotel for details of late opening hours.

Water. You can drink tap water anywhere in South Africa–even in the game parks. In some coastal areas it may be tinted by iron deposits, but it's still potable.

L

LANGUAGE

Since 1994, South Africa has recognised 11 official languages: English, Afrikaans, Zulu, Xhosa, Sotho, Venda, Tswana, Tsonga, Pedi, Shangaan and Ndebele. Most whites and people of mixed race (Coloureds) claim Afrikaans (derived from Dutch) as their mother tongue. In practice, most people understand English, but here are a few phrases you might try in an Afrikaans environment. Note that the 'g' is pronounced as a throaty 'kh', and 'oe' is pronounced 'oo'.

Good morning **Goeie môre**
Good afternoon **Goeie middag**
Good night **Goeie nag**
Please **Asseblief**
Thank you **Dankie**
Goodbye **Tot siens**

Many common Afrikaans words and expressions have been borrowed by English-speakers in South Africa:

bakkie pickup truck
braai barbecue
combi microbus or minibus
dorp small town
kop/koppie hilltop/small hill
rondavel circular hut/house
robot traffic light
tsotsi mugger, street criminal

M

MAPS
South African Tourism (see page 127) issues (free) excellent tourist maps of South Africa and the regions. Local information offices, car-hire firms and the Automobile Association (for AA members) are also sources of free maps.

MEDIA
Newspapers. There are daily newspapers in all the main cities. The national Sunday newspaper is the *Sunday Times*. Newspapers focus on South African news: it is hard to find good international coverage.
Television. The state-run SABC operates three public television channels. Many hotels also have M-Net, a subscribers-only channel, together with its multi-channel satellite subsidiary DSTV, which includes the likes of CNN, BBC World, Sky TV and MTN.
Radio. As well as some 65 community stations, the SABC transmits various services on FM, including the English Service– a mix of news, music and features; the Afrikaans Service; and Radio 5, which specialises in pop music. In addition, there are regional ser-

vices on AM and FM, and stations broadcasting in the major black languages. BBC, Voice of America and European shortwave stations can be picked up; BBC and VOA also use a medium-wave frequency for southern Africa.

MONEY

Currency. The unit of currency of South Africa is the rand (R), divided into 100 cents (c). For currency restrictions, see page 130. Coins come in denominations of 5c, 10c, 20c and 50c. Banknotes are R10, R20, R50, R100 and R200. The R200 note looks like the R20.

Credit cards and travellers' cheques. All commercial banks cash travellers' cheques in any major hard currency. Many hotels and shops also welcome travellers' cheques. Major international credit cards, especially Visa and Mastercard, are widely accepted in hotels, shops and by tour operators and carriers. Some bank branches will advance cash against a major credit card.

Taxes. VAT at a standard rate (currently 14 percent) is charged on all purchases of goods and services, except on some basic foodstuffs. It is included in the prices advertised. VAT may be reclaimed when the total value of items taken out of the country exceeds R250. For information on the refund process, visit www.taxrefunds.co.za or contact the VAT Refund Administrator's offices at both Johannesburg (O.R. Tambo) and Cape Town international airports.

O

OPENING HOURS

Business hours are typically 8.30am–5pm. Most shops are open Mon–Fri 8.30am–6pm, Sat until 12.30pm (longer in urban areas), Sun 3pm (urban areas). Some greengrocers, pharmacies, bookshops and supermarkets may stay open later. Cafés (essentially small general stores) may operate seven days a week 6am–midnight. Some big shopping centres stay open until 5pm on Saturday and until lunchtime on Sunday, others like Cape Town's V&A Waterfront open 9am–9pm, even on Sunday. Beachfront shops of all kinds in Durban stay open all day on Sunday. Banks open Monday to Friday 9am–4pm, Saturday 9am– noon (later in major cities).

P

POLICE (See also Emergencies)

The national police force, who are armed, wear blue uniforms and peaked caps. In the cities they usually drive small 'Black Maria' vans (actually yellow). The traffic police wear khaki uniforms.

POST OFFICES

Most post offices are open Mon–Fri 8.30am–4.30pm, Sat 9am–noon. Smaller offices close for lunch from 1–2pm. Mail boxes, many of them bearing the monograms of British sovereigns, are painted red. Service is reasonably fast for overseas mail.

Poste restante. If you're not sure where you'll be staying, you may have mail addressed to you *poste restante* (general delivery). The main post offices – on Parliament Street in Cape Town, West Street in Durban, Jeppe Street in Johannesburg and Church Square in Pretoria – have special counters for this service.

PUBLIC HOLIDAYS

Note that whenever a holiday falls on a Sunday, the Monday is taken as a public holiday too.

January 1 New Year's Day
March 21 Human Rights' Day
April 27 Freedom Day
May 1 Workers' Day
June 16 Youth Day
August 9 National Women's Day
September 24 Heritage Day

December 16 Day of Reconciliation
December 25/26 Xmas Day/Goodwill Day
Movable dates:
Good Friday, Family Day (Easter Monday).

T

TELEPHONES

The international access code is 09. (The country code to use in IDD calls to South Africa is 27. Dial 00 27 then drop the first digit of the area code).

Calls within South Africa are cheaper between 6pm and 8pm from Monday to Friday and cheapest between 8pm and 7am, and from 1pm on Saturday to 7am on Monday.

Directions in coin-operated telephones are given in English and Afrikaans. Phone cards in R10 denominations are available at post offices and other outlets. They can be used at green public telephones for calls within South Africa and international calls. In Johannesburg an international telephone office on the ground floor of the Post Office building in Smal Street is open 24 hours a day. Mobile phones can be hired at Johannesburg International Airport. British phones will work in South Africa but are expensive to use as calls route through the UK. Pay-as-you-go SIM cards are cheaply available at supermarkets and mobile phone shops. For 24-hour assistance call 10903.

TIME ZONES

All year round, South Africa stays on GMT + 2. There is no daylight saving time. For example, during (northern) winter:

Los Angeles	New York	London	**South Africa**	Sydney
2am	5am	10am	**noon**	9pm

TIPPING

In South Africa tipping is less generous than in most of Europe and North America. Tips are expected, but not always received, by filling station attendants, hotel maids, railway porters, taxi drivers, waiters, stewards and caddies. Some suggestions: hairdresser 10 percent; maid, per week R20–25; porter, per bag R5; taxi driver 10 percent; tour guide 10 percent; waiter 10–15 percent if service not included; car guard R3–5.

TOURIST INFORMATION

All larger towns and cities have a Tourist Information Bureau, which can be identified by a large white 'I' on a green background, and will be able to provide city maps and information. The country's nine provincial authorities all have excellent websites:

Eastern Cape Tourism: tel: 043-705 4400, www.visiteasterncape.co.za.
Free State Tourism Marketing Board: tel: 051-409 9900, www.free statetourism.org.
Gauteng Tourism Agency: tel: 011-085 2500, www.gauteng.net.
KwaZulu-Natal Tourism Authority: tel: 031-366 7500, www.zulu.org.za.
Limpopo Tourism Board: tel: 015-293 3600, www.golimpopo.com.
Mpumalanga Tourism Authority: tel: 013-759 5300, www.mpuma langa.com.
Northern Cape Tourism Authority: tel: 053-832 2657, www.experi encenortherncape.com.
North-West Parks and Tourism Authority: tel: 086-111 1866, www.tourismnorthwest.co.za.
Western Cape: tel: 021-487 8600, http://goto.capetown.

Offices run by South African Tourism providing countrywide information. The head office postal address is: Private Bag: X10012, Sandton 2146; tel: 011-895 3000, www.southafrica.net.

South African Tourism offices abroad:

Australia: Suite 302, Level 3, 117 York Street, Sydney NSW 2000;

tel: 02-9261 5000.

UK: 2nd floor, 1-2 Castle Lane, London SW1E6DR; tel: 020-8971 9350 or 08701 550044.

US: 500 Fifth Avenue, 22nd Floor, Suite 2200 New York, NY 10110; tel: 212-730 2929 or 800-593 1318.

TRANSPORT

Buses. In Johannesburg, the Rea Vaya public bus system operates weekdays from 5am to 9pm (6am–7pm at weekends) and offers regular services every 10 minutes (every 15 minutes during off-peak hours and every 30 minutes at weekends). Top-up smart cards can be bought at the following stations across town: Orlando Stadium, Diepkloof, UJ Kingsway, Park Station, Johannesburg Art Gallery and Carlton Centre. Alternatively, you can buy a single/double trip card. For details, visit the website www.reavaya.org.za. A similar system called MyCiTi (http://myciti.org.za) operates in Cape Town. Meanwhile, Durban are developing the ultra-modern GO!Durban (www.godurban.co.za) public transport system, which will be completed by 2030. Besides the ordinary municipal bus system, the brightly-coloured People Mover buses take tourists through the main city thoroughfares and to the northern and southern city beaches. Buses run every 15 minutes between 5am–10pm and are accessible to wheelchair users. Bus-stop wardens offer help to disabled passengers. For detailed information on public transport in Durban, see www.durban.gov.za.

Trains. Many South African trains are fascinating. Hundreds of steam locomotives still earn their keep. Several narrow-gauge lines still operate. At the other end of the scale the Blue Train (see page 82), the pride of South African Railways, maintains five-star luxury between Pretoria and Cape Town. All long-distance trains have sleeping compartments in first and second class. For details visit www.railtravel.co.za.

Flights. For internal flights, try budget airlines: South African Airlink (http://flyairlink.com), Kulula (www.kulula.com), Mango (www.flyman

go.com) or South African Express (ww.flyexpress.aero). Traditional airlines such as South African Airways (www.flysaa.com) or British Airways (www.britishairways.com) also offer regular domestic flights.

Taxis. In South African cities the taxis do not normally cruise for fares. Go to a taxi rank or ask your hotel to call a cab. In Johannesburg taxis are usually found outside the Carlton Centre in Kruis Street. In Cape Town a likely taxi rank is opposite the train station in Lower Adderley Street. The word taxi also applies to the many minibuses which ply fixed routes. Fares vary from town to town – meters start at about R10 (R35 in Pretoria), plus R10–15 per km. The minimum fare is R20 plus tip.

TRAVELLERS WITH DISABILITIES

Great advances have been made in recent years in the provision of special toilet facilities and wheelchair access to public buildings, hotels and other places visitors might want to go. South African Tourism's accommodation brochure (see page 111), gives details of these facilities, and the Independent Living Institute, www.independentliving.org, can also advise you on specific facilities and services.

V

VISAS AND ENTRY REQUIREMENTS

Passport holders from most EU countries (including the UK) and US, Canada, Australia and New Zealand do not require a visa for stays of up to 90 days (30 days for some EU states). However, as visa regulations are subject to change, it is wise to check with your travel agent or the nearest South African embassy or consulate. Alternatively, you can check online at www.vfsglobal.com/dha/southafrica.

If you require a visa allow plenty of time for the application to be processed. If you plan to include a visit to any neighbouring countries and then return to South Africa, you should include this information on your application so that you receive a multiple-entry visa.

Currency restrictions. Visitors should declare amounts over $10,000 upon arrival. The South African currency you may carry in is limited to R25,000.

W

WEBSITES AND INTERNET ACCESS

Useful websites covering South Africa include the following:
www.africageographic.com Wildlife and ecological magazine.
www.anc.org.za Plenty of coverage of contemporary issues.
www.coasttocoast.co.za Backpacker hostels and related facilities.
www.getaway.co.za Popular travel magazine.
www.mg.co.za The *Mail& Guardian* newspaper online.
www.wineonaplatter.com Popular wine guide.
www.sanparks.org Information and booking for national parks.
www.southafrica.net Official site of South African Tourism.
www.timeslive.co.za Good news and sport coverage.
www.womensnet.org.za Women's issues in South Africa.

Internet facilities and email are widely available in most towns, both at tourist hotels and at internet cafés, but may not be found in game reserves and other more remote areas. Some cafés in larger towns offer free Wi-Fi. AlwaysOn (www.alwayson.co.za) offers pre-paid Wi-Fi access in Cape Town, Durban, hotel chains (City Lodge, Sun International Hotels) and Mugg & Bean restaurants.

Y

YOUTH HOSTELS

For full information, check out the website of Hostelling International South Africa (HISA), www.hihostels.com. The last 10 years has seen a burgeoning growth in the number of private hostels and other facilities catering mainly to backpackers. Most are listed and reviewed in the free booklet *Coast to Coast* and related website ww.coasttocoast.co.za.

RECOMMENDED HOTELS

In the following pages we offer a short selection of establishments in the areas covered in the Where to Go section of this book (and in the same order). The list is by no means exhaustive, but is designed to give you a few pointers by selecting places which offer something extra in the way of facilities, location, character, or value for money. For a brief guide to the camps in the Kruger National Park, see page 42.

Our ratings are an indication of the cost per person, sharing a double room, with breakfast. Many country retreats and game lodges only publish rates for dinner, bed and breakfast, however. Note that there may be very wide seasonal variations, and these prices are only approximate.

$$$$	over R1,000
$$$	R500–1,000
$$	R350–500
$	under R350

GAUTENG

JOHANNESBURG

Airport Grand Hotel $$$ *100 North Rand Road, tel: 011-823 1843.* Less than 10 minutes' drive from O.R. Tambo Airport and linked to it by a regular shuttle service, this is a bland but good-value hotel for short stopovers, with a useful location opposite East Rand Mall and its numerous shops, restaurants and cinemas.

54 on Bath Hotel $$$$ *54 Bath Ave, Rosebank 2196, tel: 011-344 8500.* Luxury boutique hotel with spacious and elegantly decorated rooms in black and white and a handy location for the shopping and night-life facilities in and around Rosebank Mall. Highly rated restaurant and great buffet breakfast

Sandton Sun Hotel $$$$ *Corner Fifth Street and Alice Lane, PO Box 784902, Sandton 2196, tel: 011-780 5000/461 9744, www.tsogosun. com.* This opulent five-star tower block is probably the largest hotel in Gauteng, with a rather impersonal atmosphere compensated for by its stylishly modern decor and handy location in the heart of Sandton. Part of Sandton City, a vast shopping mall with an excellent selection of upmarket shops, cinemas and restaurants. Wi-Fi in all rooms. parking. 334 rooms.

The Saxon $$$$ *36 Saxon Road, Sandhurst, Sandton, tel: 011-292 6000,* www.thesaxon.com. In a similar class to the nearby Sandton Towers but far more characterful and intimate in feel, this prestigious Sandton hideout is favoured by celebrities and politicians. The individually decorated suites are the size of aircraft hangars, and come with all mod cons. Besides the main building there are additional private villas. The high-class decor and cuisine reflect the hotel's African setting.

Town Lodge $$$ *Herman Road, Harmelia Ext 2, Germiston, tel: 011-974 5202,* https://clhg.com. This functional hotel lies only 5km (3 miles) from O.R. Tambo International Airport, to which it is linked by a regular shuttle bus service. Air-conditioned rooms with TV and shower. 135 rooms. Facilities for disabled people.

The Four Season Hotel Westcliff $$$$ *67 Jan Smuts Avenue, Saxonworld 2132, tel: 011-481 6000,* www.fourseasons.com/johannesburg. This ultra-luxurious modern hotel is perched on a ridge close to the popular, well-equipped suburb of Rosebank, and enjoys spectacular views over the city. Features a spa, gym, swimming pool and five venues for eating and drinking. 117 rooms.

PRETORIA

StayEasy Hotel $$-$$$ *632 Lilian Ngoyi Street/Van der Walt street, Pretoria 0002, tel: (012) 407 0600;* www.tsogosun.com/stayeasy-pretoria. This modern and affordable hotel away of the city centre offers a good range of business facilities, is also suitable for leisure travellers. Buffet-style breakfast and an outdoor pool are added bonuses. 136 rooms.

Sheraton Pretoria Hotel & Towers $$$$ *Corner Stanza Bopape (Church) and Wessels streets, Arcadia, tel: 012-429 9999,* www.sheratonpretoria. com. Probably the largest hotel in the city centre, the Sheraton Pretoria also boasts a great location overlooking the Union Buildings and an excellent range of facilities including a swimming pool, two restaurants, bar, sauna, beauty salon and jewellery shop. 175 rooms.

SUN CITY

Kwa Maritane Bush Lodge $$$$ *Pilanesberg Game Reserve, tel: 014-552-5100/011-806 6888,* www.legacyhotels.co.za. This well-established game lodge in the Pilanesberg has a genuine bush feel despite its proximity to Sun City, making it an excellent base for game drives. Facilities include pools, tennis courts and a children's playground. 90 rooms and 54 self-catering chalets.

The Palace of the Lost City $$$$ *PO Box 308, Sun City Resort 0316, tel: 011-780 7855/014 557 5307,* www.suninternational.com. Extravagant hotel set in the vast, exotic resort of Sun City, which features casino, health centre, pools, golf, tennis. 338 rooms.

MADIKWE GAME RESERVE

Mosetlha Bush Camp $$$$ *PO Box 78690, Sandton 2146, tel: 011-444 9345,* www.thebushcamp.com. This rustic unfenced bush camp accommodates a maximum of 16 people in 9 double cabins, and is ideally suited to those who want a real wilderness experience at reasonable rates. Includes all meals and game drives.

Tau Game Lodge $$$$ *PO Box 1450, Halfway House 1685, tel: 011-466 8715,* www.taugamelodge.co.za. This classy lodge consists of 30 thatched chalets set in a semi-circle around a vast natural waterhole that attracts a variety of game. The dining area and bar also overlook the waterhole, while facilities include a good curio shop and swimming pool. Rates are inclusive of meals, game drives, guided walks and other activities.

MPUMALANGA AND LIMPOPO PROVINCES

Hazyview Protea $$$$ *On the R40 road, Hazyview, Mpumalanga 1242, tel: 013-737 9700,* www.marriott.com. Just 20 minutes' drive from the Kruger National Park, several private reserves and the scenic Blyde River Canyon, this hilltop lodge is set in a 10-acre country estate with attractive bird-filled gardens and fine views. Pool, tennis, sauna, games room, game drives and other activities. 83 rooms and 4 suites.

Inyathi Game Lodge $$$$ *Sabi Sand Reserve, Mpumalanga PO Box 9, Skukuza 1350, tel: 013 735 5125;* www.inyati.co.za. Situated in the western sector of the Sabi Sands Game Reserve, this lodge overlooking the Sand River offers a classic luxury safari experience. 11 luxury en-suite chalets, morning and evening game drives, pool, gym, cocktail bar, wine cellar.

Londolozi Game Reserve $$$$ *Sabi Sand Reserve, PO Box 6, Skukuza 1350, tel: 011-280 6655,* www.londolozi.com. Known for its top-range quality, comfort and service. Escorted drives/walks in bush. Highly rated for leopard sightings, but good for other predators and the big five. Five private camps and one safari lodge.

MalaMala Game Reserve $$$$ *Sabi Sand Reserve, via Skukuza 1353, PO Box 55514, Northlands 2116, tel: 011-442 2267/73 621 1289,* www.malamala.com. Luxurious game lodge with chalets in an idyllic setting and excellent game drives and guided walks led by experienced game rangers on staff. Has its own airstrip – you can fly here from Johannesburg.

Mount Sheba Country Lodge $$$-$$$$ *above Pilgrim's Rest, PO Box 100, Pilgrim's Rest 1290, tel: 013-768 1241/012 423 5600,* www.mount-sheba.co.za. 26 rooms in their own nature reserve. Hilltop and forest setting, thatched stone houses. Pool, walks, birdwatching.

Ngala Game Lodge $$$$ *Timbavati Game Reserve, reservations through &Beyond, tel: 011-809 4300,* www.andbeyond.com. 20 luxury thatched chalets, pool. Rangers escort walks and drives through the bush. Perfect for families with children.

Sabi River Sun $$$$ *Main Sabie Road, PO Box 13, Hazyview Mpumalanga 1242, tel: 013 737 4600,* www.tsogosun.com/sabi-river-sun-resort. Luxury hotel located close to the Kruger National Park. Golf course, swimming pools, spa, squash and tennis courts. 60 rooms.

Sabi Sabi Game Reserve $$$$ *Sabi Sand Reserve, Skukuza 1350, tel: 011-447 7172,* www.sabisabi.com. These luxury lodges are situated amid a big-game area bordering the Kruger National Park. Rangers take you on day and night safaris. 52 rooms.

Thornybush Game Reserve $$$$ *Corner Rivonia Village and Mutual Road, tel: 011-253 6500,* www.thornybush.co.za. Beautifully appointed thatched chalets and pool overlook bush. Day walks are escorted by rangers. There is a wide range of game.

UKHAHLAMBA-DRAKENSBERG

Ardmore Guest Farm $$$ *PO Box 122, Champagne Valley, Winterton 3340, tel: 087 997 1194,* www.ardmore.co.za. Small owner-managed guesthouse on grassy green farmland, overshadowed by the peaks of Champagne Castle. Superb home-cooked five-course meals. Reasonably priced and includes breakfast.

Cathedral Peak Hotel $$$$ *Near Winterton, KwaZulu-Natal 3340, tel: 036-488 1888,* www.cathedralpeak.co.za. Built in the 1930s by the same family that manages it today, this is the only private hotel set within the uKhahlamba-Drakensberg Park and it makes a fine base for walking and visits to the nearby Didima Rock Art Centre. Thatched cottages and suites, pool, tennis, bowls, squash, bike riding and fishing. 104 rooms.

Champagne Sports Resort $$$ *Private Bag X9, Winterton 3340, tel: 036-468 8000,* www.champagnesportsresort.com. This recently extended, sprawling resort straddles the R600 to Monk's Cowl in the central uKhahlamba-Drakensberg and is better suited to sports enthusiasts than to hikers, with a popular golf course as well as bowls, squash, tennis, gym, volleyball, and a swimming pool. The hotel rooms and thatched cottages all come with heating and satellite TV. 152 rooms and 91 chalets.

Orion Mont-Aux-Sources Hotel $$$$ *Private bag X1670, Bergville, KwaZulu-Natal 3350, tel: 036-438 8000/086-148 8867,* www.montaux sources.co.za. Situated 5 minutes' drive from the entrance to Royal Natal National Park, this stalwart hotel boasts arguably the most scenic setting of any accommodation in the uKhahlamba-Drakensberg. It also has good sports facilities, a popular restaurant, and superb hiking possibilities.

DURBAN AND KWAZULU-NATAL COAST

Blue Marlin $$$ *180, Scott Street, Scottburgh 4180, tel: 039-978 3361,* www.bluemarlinhotel.co.za. This is a popular and well-priced multi-storey beach resort set in sprawling green grounds about 50km (30 miles) south of Durban. In addition to the usual seaside activities, the hotel arranges scuba dives and lies within 20 minutes' drive of four highly rated golf courses. 122 en-suite rooms with ceiling fan and satellite TV. Prices are all inclusive.

Oyster Box Hotel $$$$ *2 Lighthouse Road, Umhlanga Rocks, Natal 4319, tel: 31 514 5000,* www.oysterboxhotel.com. Founded in 1920, this legendary beachfront hotel is set in tropical gardens in sight of the Umhlanga lighthouse, on the coast north of Durban. The plentiful facilities include a Turkish bath, dolphin watching and a small cinema, and the restaurant is top-notch. 86 rooms.

Protea Hotel Edward $$$$ *149 O.R. Tambo Parade (Marine Parade), Durban 4001, tel: 031-337 3681,* www.marriott.com. Founded in 1911, this white multi-storey block on the Golden Mile seafront retains a classic Victorian ambience and has good facilities and a perfect location for beach lovers. 131 rooms.

The Royal Hotel $$$-$$$$ *267 Anton Lembede Street (Smith Street), Durban 4000, tel: 031-333 6000,* www.theroyal.co.za. More than a century old but immaculately maintained and fully modernised, this luxurious hotel in central Durban is widely regarded to be the city's most prestigious address. Facilities include a swimming pool, squash courts, health club, airport transfers, business centre, and internet, and there's plenty of choice when it comes to dining, with six restaurants and two cocktail bars on the property. 251 rooms.

ZULULAND

Hilltop Camp $$$ *Hluhluwe iMfolozi Game Reserve, tel: 035-208 3684,* www.hilltopcamp.co.za. Modern motel-like rest camp with 70 en-suite chalets and huts offering expansive views across green hills dotted with wildlife.

Kingfisher Lodge $$$ *187 McKenzie Street, PO Box 291, St Lucia Village 3936, tel: 035-590 1015,* www.stluciakingfisherlodge.co.za. Smart six-suites B&B set in lush gardens on St Lucia Estuary – great for birds, hippos and duikers.

Mpila Camp $-$$$ *Imfolozi Game Reserve, tel: 031-208 368/035-550 8476.* www.mpilacamp.co.za. Rustic self-catering camp whose elevated safari tents regularly receive nocturnal visits from spotted hyena, porcupine and other small carnivores. No restaurant, and the small shop has limited supplies.

Phinda Resource Reserve $$$$ *near Mkhuze, Natal, reservations through &Beyond, tel: 011-809 4300,* www.andbeyond.com. Five luxury Big Five game lodges in river and forest settings, offering 4x4 excursions and walking safaris.

Shakaland $$$$ *Normanhurst Farm, Nkwalini Zululand 3816, tel: 035-460 0912/087 740 9292,* http://aha.co.za/shakaland. Commodious ensuite traditional beehive huts with fans complement an excellent Zulu cultural programme that starts at 4pm for overnight visitors.

Zulu Nyala Lodge $$$ *PO Box 163, Hluhluwe 3960, tel: 035-562 0177/ 011-702 9300,* www.zulunyalagroup.com. This private game reserve adjacent to Phinda supports many of the same species. Luxury tented camps, including guided 4x4 drives and good food.

EASTERN CAPE AND GARDEN ROUTE

Bitou River Lodge $$$ *PO Box 491, Plettenberg Bay 6600, tel: 044-535 9577,* www.bitou.co.za. This charming owner-managed lodge consists of just five rooms set along the forested banks of the Bitou River – canoes available – about 10km (6 miles) from Plettenberg Bay.

Eight Bells Mountain Inn $$$ *PO Box 436, Mossel Bay 6500, tel: 044-631 0000,* www.eightbells.co.za. Family-run country inn set amid stunning mountain scenery halfway between Mossel Bay and Oudtshoorn. Wide variety of sports facilities, including squash, tennis, bowls and a swimming pool.

The Grand Café and Rooms $$$$ *27 Main Road, Plettenberg Bay, tel: 044-533 3301*, http://grandafrica.com. Quirky opulence is what to expect here, with decadent rooms overlooking the ocean and mountains. Breakfast room and pool courtyard exclusively for guests; dinner for non-guests too.

King Edward $$$ *Belmont Terrace, Port Elizabeth 6001, tel: 078-137 2907*. Centrally located hotel in the historic district. Re-opened in 2015 after five years of refurbishment. Overlooks the bay. 104 rooms.

Phantom Forest Lodge $$$$ *Phantom Pass, PO Box 3051, Knysna 6570, tel: 044-386 0046*, http://phantomforest.com. Set in a private nature reserve, these luxury treehouses are made of entirely natural materials and have huge bathrooms with underfloor heating. Choose between Moroccan or contemporary cuisine at two restaurants. Food and service are both excellent. There is also a spa.

The Plettenberg $$$$ *40 Church Street, PO Box 719, Plettenberg Bay 6600, tel: 044-533 2030*, www.collectionmcgrath.com. Luxurious resort overlooking the sea with the top notch restaurant. Swimming pool. 35 rooms.

Shamwari Game Reserve $$$$ *6130 Paterson, Eastern Cape, tel: 042-203 1111*, www.shamwari.com. Award-winning private game reserve near Addo, with superior accommodation inclusive of guided game drives that offer the opportunity to see the Big Five and African wild dogs.

CAPE TOWN AND CAPE PENINSULA

The Cellars-Hohenort $$$$ *93 Brommersvlei Road, Constantia, Cape Town 7806, tel: 021-794 2137*, www.collectionmcgrath.com. Graceful hotel converted from the 18th-century cellars of the former Klaasenbosch wine farm. Set in large landscaped gardens. Facilities include two pools, tennis and golf. Close to Kirstenbosch.

Lord Nelson Inn $$-$$$ *58 St George's Street, False Bay, Simon's Town 7995, tel: 021-786 1386*, www.lordnelsoninn.co.za. This reasonably priced inn-like hotel is set in an agreeable location on Simon's Town waterfront and has just 10 rooms.

Majoro's Bed and Breakfast $ *69 Helena Crescent, Graceland, Khaye-litsha, Cape Town, tel: 082-537 6882.* Traditional African experience, complete with trip to a local township.

Belmond Mount Nelson $$$$ *76 Orange Street, Cape Town 8001, tel: 021-483 1000,* www.belmond.com. The legendary 'Nellie' ranks among the country's most prestigious and luxurious hotels. It is set in spacious landscaped gardens at the northern end of the city centre, in the shadow of gorgeous Table Mountain. Pools, gym, tennis, squash and several superb restaurants. 201 rooms.

The Peninsula $$$$ *313 Beach Road, Sea Point, Cape Town 8061, tel: 021-430 7777,* www.peninsula.co.za. The Peninsula is a luxurious all-suite tower block with a superb seafront location within walking distance of the city centre. Pool, health centre, gym, business facilities. 110 rooms.

Twelve Apostles Hotel $$$$ *Victoria Road, Camps Bay, tel: 021-437 9000,* www.12apostleshotel.com. Since it opened in 2003, this boutique hotel has been hot-listed in *Condé Nast Traveller* and *Travel and Leisure*, while *GQ* named it 'Hotel with the Best View in the World' – with food, service and ambience to match. 70 rooms and suits.

The Vineyard Hotel and Spa $$$$ *Colinton Road (off Protea Road), PO Box 151, Newlands 7700, Cape Town, tel: 021-657 4500,* www.vineyard.co.za. Built in 1799, this beautifully restored country-house hotel lies in landscaped gardens in the leafy upmarket suburb of Newlands. Heated pool, health and fitness centre, two highly rated restaurant. 207 rooms.

CAPE WINELANDS

Oude Werf $$$$ *30 Church Street, Stellenbosch 7600, tel: 021-887 4608,* www.oudewerfhotel.co.za. Founded in 1802, this elegantly restored old country inn has a wonderful ambience and an ideal location for exploring the historic heart of Stellenbosch and its plethora of quaint restaurants and wine cellars. Pool, gardens. 58 rooms.

Grande Roche $$$$ *Plantasie Street 1, PO Box 6038, Paarl 7620, tel: 021-863 5100,* www.granderoche.com. Former historic Cape Dutch farm buildings converted into luxury suites. Two highly rated restaurants lie on the property. Pools, tennis, gym, outdoor theatre. 34 rooms and suites.

De Wingerd Wijnland Lodge $$$ *7 Waltham Cross Street, Paarl 7646, tel: 021-868; 1994;* www.wingerd.co.za. Located in a quiet residential area, the De Wingerd Wijnland Lodge offers 4 spacious en-suite rooms and 1 luxurious cottage, which boast breath-taking views of the Grande Roche vineyards, Paarl valley and the majestic Hottentots Mountains. There is a large swimming pool and a beautiful garden. An excellent breakfast included.

NORTHERN CAPE

Garden Court Kimberley $$$$ *120 Du Toitspan Road, PO Box 635, Kimberley 8300, tel: 011-461 9744;* www.southernsun.com. Luxurious resort and business hotel. Pool, sauna, state-of-the-art gym and meeting facilities. 135 rooms.

Berlitz POCKET GUIDE

SOUTH AFRICA

Sixth Edition 2017

Editor: Tom Fleming
Author: Martin Gostelow and Ken Bernstein
Head of Production: Rebeka Davies
Picture Editor: Tom Smyth
Cartography Update: Carte
Update Production: AM Services
Photography Credits: Alex Havret/Apa
Publications 5MC, 7M, 74, 97, 103; Ariadne
Van Zandbergen/Apa Publications ; 4TC, 4MC,
4ML, 5T, 5TC, 5M, 6TC, 7T, 7MC, 7T, 8L, 8R,
9, 9R, 10, 13, 20, 24, 26, 29, 30, 32, 34, 37, 46,
47, 51, 52, 59, 62, 63, 64, 65, 67, 68, 71, 72, 75,
77, 79, 80, 84, 86, 88, 91, 93, 94, 98, 101; Ethos
Marketing 5MC; Getty Images 4TL, 5M, 17,
23, 28, 38, 55, 61; Inyathi Game Lodge 6TL,
6ML; iStock 43, 44, 49; Robert Harding 50;
Shutterstock 6ML, 15, 19, 40, 56, 83
Cover Picture: Shutterstock

Distribution
UK, Ireland and Europe: Apa Publications
(UK) Ltd; sales@insightguides.com
United States and Canada: Ingram Publisher
Services; ips@ingramcontent.com
Australia and New Zealand: Woodslane;
info@woodslane.com.au
Southeast Asia: Apa Publications (SN) Pte;
singaporeoffice@insightguides.com
Hong Kong, Taiwan and China:
Apa Publications (HK) Ltd;
hongkongoffice@insightguides.com
Worldwide: Apa Publications (UK) Ltd;
sales@insightguides.com

**Special Sales, Content Licensing
and CoPublishing**
Insight Guides can be purchased in bulk
quantities at discounted prices. We can create
special editions, personalised jackets and
corporate imprints tailored to your needs.
sales@insightguides.com;
www.insightguides.biz

All Rights Reserved
© 2017 Apa Digital (CH) AG and
Apa Publications (UK) Ltd

Printed in China by CTPS

No part of this book may be reproduced,
stored in a retrieval system or transmitted in
any form or means electronic, mechanical,
photocopying, recording or otherwise,
without prior written permission from Apa
Publications.

Contact us
Every effort has been made to provide
accurate information in this publication,
but changes are inevitable. The publisher
cannot be responsible for any resulting loss,
inconvenience or injury. We would appreciate
it if readers would call our attention to any
errors or outdated information. We also
welcome your suggestions; please contact us
at: berlitz@apaguide.co.uk
www.insightguides.com/berlitz

Berlitz Trademark Reg. U.S. Patent Office
and other countries. Marca Registrada.
Used under licence from the Berlitz
Investment Corporation

Berlitz®

speaking your language

phrase book & dictionary
phrase book & CD

Available in: Arabic, Brazilian Portuguese*, Burmese*, Cantonese
Chinese, Croatian, Czech*, Danish*, Dutch, English, Filipino, Finnish*, French,
German, Greek*, Hebrew*, Hindi*, Hungarian*, Indonesian, Italian, Japanese,
Korean, Latin American Spanish, Malay, Mandarin Chinese, Mexican Spanish,
Norwegian, Polish, Portuguese, Romanian*, Russian, Spanish, Swedish, Thai,
Turkish, Vietnamese
*Book only

www.berlitzpublishing.com